Gospel
Sermons
for
Children

Gospel Sermons *for* Children

*60 Creative and Easy-to-Use
Messages on Gospel Texts*

Augsburg
MINNEAPOLIS

GOSPEL SERMONS FOR CHILDREN
Gospels, Series A

Scripture quotations are from the New Revised Standard Version Bible, copyright © 1989 by the Division of Christian Education of the National Council of Churches of Christ in the United States of America. Used with permission.

Cover design: Cindy Cobb Olson
Interior design: Craig Claeys

Library of Congress Cataloging-in-Publication Data

Gospel Sermons for Children
  p. cm.
  [1] Gospels, series A
  ISBN 0-8066-2780-8 (v. 1)
  1. Bible. N.T. Gospels—Sermons. 2. Children's sermons. 3. Church year sermons.
4. Lutheran Church—Sermons 5. Sermons, American. I. Augsburg Fortress (Publisher)
BS2555.4.G67 1995
252'.53—dc20

          95-10471
          CIP

Manufactured in the U.S.A.   AF9-2780

99   98   97   96   95   1   2   3   4   5   6   7   8   9   10

Contents

WILLIAM YOUNGKIN, PASTOR
DAVID'S UNITED CHURCH OF CHRIST
KETTERING, OHIO

LORI ROSENKVIST, WRITER
TOFTE, MINNESOTA

DON HOWARD, DIRECTOR OF CHRISTIAN EDUCATION
HOLY CROSS LUTHERAN CHURCH
LAWTON, OKLAHOMA

DON HOWARD

Preface

Gospel Messages for Children brings you sixty new children's sermons which the publishers hope will help both the leaders and the children understand the Gospel. The popularity of the three volumes published earlier (*Augsburg Sermons for Children*, one volume each for the Gospel texts for series A, B, and C) led to this new series. We hope these continue to communicate God's love to God's children.

Having a children's sermon is not the only way to let children know they are included in the worship service, but it is a good way. During this special time, the stories and messages from the Gospels can be communicated to children in ways they can understand. We need to remind ourselves that children are full members of the household of faith. The fact that their concerns, interests, and levels of understanding are taken seriously through these children's sermons is an indication that they are taken seriously. Even though the messages use simple language and basic concepts, the Gospel comes through clearly.

The Gospel texts are taken primarily from the *Revised Common Lectionary* which is used in the worship services of a number of denominations. The Gospel texts for series A are mostly from Matthew. If there was a choice of readings for a Sunday, the ones designated as Lutheran were selected in most cases. Notice that for the Sundays in Pentecost, the word *Proper* and the appropriate number are given. Because the proper texts for the Sundays in Pentecost are determined by the date of Trinity Sunday, the dates when each of the Gospel texts will be used are given at the top of the page for the years 1996, 1999, and 2002. Churches following a free-text tradition may use the sermons whenever they meet their needs. In this volume, a children's sermon for Thanksgiving is included, using the suggested revised lectionary text.

The introductory material for each of the sermons provides helpful information for you as leader. After the name of the Sunday and the reference for the Gospel text, these follow:

— *Focus.* A brief statement of the theme.

— *Experience.* What you and the children will be doing.

— *Preparation.* What needs to be done ahead of time.

Some of the children's sermons use objects or special arrangements. However, these sermons are not the traditional kind of object lessons that ask children to make symbolic connections between an object and a spiritual concept. Abstract, symbolic thinking is beyond most children's ability.

When an object or prop is part of a sermon, let the children hold it or help you with it. They will learn more from their own experience than from simply watching you. Asking a couple of children to help you lay out a paper road or use a tape measure helps them to feel needed and important.

As you plan to present these children's sermons, you will bring your own style and gifts to them. Your own creativity, spontaneity, and flexibility will give energy to the messages. Children usually are eager to join in such experiences, and your enthusiasm will help them want to participate.

Your primary audience will be the children who come forward, but other children who are too hesitant or shy to participate will listen and watch. Adult and youth will also be interested in what happens and may remember the main point of the children's sermon longer than other parts of the service.

Whenever you can, include open-ended questions. Asking the children, "What do you worry about?" will lead to more interesting responses than "Do you ever worry?" A few short-answer questions do not need to be ruled out; they can serve well to set the stage for an activity.

These children's sermons emphasize grace more than law. That is not to say that there is no emphasis on how to live. That is there, but always in the context that we are already loved. As much as possible, these messages communicate how God shows grace through Jesus Christ; how God worked through the lives of people in Bible times, throughout the centuries, and today; and how much God loves each of the children.

First Sunday in Advent

The Gospel: Matthew 24:37-44

Focus: We need to get ready for Jesus.

Experience: After discussing how they prepare for the return of their parent(s), the children will think of ways that they can prepare for the return of Jesus.

Getting Ready

WELCOME! I'M GLAD YOU'RE HERE. Raise your hand if you've ever had a baby-sitter come to your home to take care of you while your mom or dad was away. *(Address the next question to the children whose hands are raised.)* What do you like to do while the babysitter is at your home? *(Give them time to share.)*

Usually before they leave, moms or dads tell the baby-sitter about certain things that you kids should do. What do your moms and dads tell the babysitter that you should do? *(Pick up toys, go to bed at a certain time, other responses.)* You know that your mom and dad love you, but how do they feel if they come home and you haven't *(name some of the instructions the children gave as examples)*? *(Sad, angry, disappointed.)* So what do you need to do to make sure that your mom or dad will be pleased when they return? *(Do what they said to do. Parents are pleased when their instructions are followed.)*

Today is the first Sunday in Advent. Do you know what Advent is? *(Help them realize it's the time when Christians get ready for Christmas; four weeks long.)* Jesus was born on that first Christmas. Years later, he died, he rose from the dead, and he went up to heaven. Jesus loves us so much, and he also gave us some instructions for how we should live. Where can we find the words about how much he loves us and also those instructions? *(The Bible.)*

Today's Gospel reading tells us that Jesus is going to come back to earth some day. It tells us to be ready. During Advent Christians remember that Jesus is coming again. If we want our parents to be pleased when they come home, what do we need to do? *(Do what they tell us to do.)* What are some things that we could be doing to show Jesus that we love him so that he will be pleased when he returns? *(Some possible answers: love and help other people, trust God, pray, read the Bible, tell people that Jesus loves and forgives them, and believe that Jesus is our Savior.)*

Let's pray. Jesus, thank you for coming to us that first Christmas. Help us to *(name the ways the children just mentioned)* while we wait for you to come again. Amen.. — **C. S.**

The Gospel: Matthew 3:1-12

Focus: We are getting ready for Jesus.

Experience: After figuring out what to do so that the king can travel down the paper road to their house, the children will think of ways to get themselves ready for Jesus.

Preparation: Cut a long strip of paper (or tape papers together) to represent a road. Bring a large box for the king's house, a small box for our house, and pencils or dowels to represent fallen trees. Decorate a large envelope. Place an official-looking letter in it that says: "I am coming to your house. Love, the King."

The King Is Coming!

HI! I'M GOING TO TELL YOU A STORY ABOUT A ROAD, so we'll need to make room for the road. *(Rearrange the children, making room for the paper road through the middle of the group. Put the road in place.)*

Once upon a time there was a road. At this end of the road lived a king. *(Place the king's box at one end.)* Our house is at the other end. *(Place the smaller box at the other end of the road.)* One night there was a big storm. The high winds blew down some trees. They fell right on the road. *(Drop the pencils or dowels onto the road.)*

One day an important letter arrived at our house. *(Show the letter. Invite a child who reads to read it aloud: "I am coming to your house. Love, the King.")* How do you think we feel when we find out that the king is coming to our house? *(Excited, nervous, happy.)* Suddenly we remember the big storm and wonder if the king will be able to travel all the way down the road to our house. So we walk down the road to take a look. What problem do we see? *(The trees.)* What can we do? *(When they suggest moving the trees, ask a couple of children to pile the trees by the side of the road.)* That's better. Now the king will be able to get to our house.

Jesus, our king, wants to come into our lives. During Advent we get ready for Jesus. We try to get rid of those things that block the road to our hearts, things like being mean, taking things from others, being selfish. These things are called sins.

What are some of the things you've done that were wrong? *(Responses.)* What are some good things that you should have done, but didn't?

(Responses.) God will help us to stop doing things that are wrong and help us to do good things. We know that God forgives us for our sins.

Now let's pray. God, we're sorry for these sins. Thank you for forgiving our sins. Thank you for clearing the road to our hearts so that Jesus can come in. Amen. **— C. S.**

The Gospel: Matthew 11:2-11

Focus: We tell other people about Jesus.

Experience: After using clues to figure out who their visitor is going to be, the children will think of what they could tell others so that they too would recognize Jesus.

Preparation: Arrange for someone known by a majority of the children to enter the room when asked. Think of clues that describe this person's personality and activities. For example: She smiles a lot. She sings in the choir. She teaches the kindergarten class in Sunday school.

Who Is Coming?

GOOD MORNING! IN JUST A MINUTE, someone is going to come into this room. I'm going to give you some clues. Let's see if you can guess who's coming. *(Give the clues. Let the children guess who is coming. Ask the person to come in.)* How did you know it was going to be *(name of person who entered)*? *(The children will probably repeat some of the clues you gave them.)*

During Advent, we get ourselves ready for someone who's coming. Who's coming? *(Jesus.)* Suppose someone didn't know Jesus. What could we do to help them know who Jesus is? *(We could tell them what Jesus is like.)* That's right. We can tell other people what Jesus did and said. What would you tell someone about Jesus? *(He is kind and loving, he likes children, he fed people, he healed people, he died on a cross, he became alive again, other responses.)*

Let's pray. Thank you, Jesus, for *(mention some comments the children shared about Jesus)*. Help us to tell other people about you. Amen. **— C. S.**

The Gospel: Matthew 1:18-25

Focus: Jesus' name tells us why God sent Jesus.

Experience: The children will learn the meanings of some of their names. They will hear the story of how Jesus was named and think about why Jesus was given that name.

Preparation: Bring a baby name book. Look up the meaning of your name. Check to see if Jesus is included in the book.

Naming Jesus

HI! ADVENT IS THE TIME WHEN WE LOOK FORWARD to celebrating the birth of a special baby sent by God. Who was that baby? *(Jesus.)* Raise your hand if you're waiting for a baby to be born in your family or a relative's family, maybe a sister or a brother or a cousin. *(Ask several of those whose hands are raised the next three questions. If no hands were raised, skip over these questions.)* What is the new baby going to be named? Who picked the name? Why was that name chosen?

(Hold up the baby name book.) Some of your parents may have used a book like this one to choose your name. Did you know that names have meanings? *(Pause.)* My first name's *(your name)* and it means *(the meaning)*. Do any of you know the meaning of your name? *(Give those who know a chance to share. Look up the meanings of a few of the children's names.)*

Today's Gospel story told how Jesus got his name. Did Mary and Joseph choose a name out of a baby name book? *(The children may shake their heads, say no, or tell you what happened. If they tell what happened, skip the next question.)* How did Jesus get his name? *(An angel of the Lord appeared to Joseph in a dream and told him to name the baby Jesus. If the children don't know, tell them.)* Why did the angel say that the baby should be named Jesus? *(If the children don't remember, tell them that the baby was to be named Jesus because he would save his people from their sins.)* In Hebrew, the name Jesus means "God is help" or "God is my salvation." *(If Jesus is in your book, find the meaning and invite a child who can read to read it aloud.)*

God gave Jesus a name that told what Jesus was going to do—help us by saving us from our sins.

Let's pray. Forgive us, God, when we do things we know we shouldn't do or when we don't do things we know we should do. Thank you for sending Jesus to save us from our sins. Amen. **— C. S.**

The Gospel: Luke 2:1-20

Focus: We can praise God for sending Jesus as our Savior.

Experience: The children will imagine what it was like to be one of the shepherds visited by the angels. They will praise God for sending Jesus for everyone.

Preparation: Bring pictures or Christmas cards that show shepherds and sheep out in the fields and shepherds visiting the baby in the manger. Choose a Christmas carol or song of praise that most of the children know. If you feel uncomfortable leading songs, invite someone to help you.

Jesus Is for Everyone

EACH CHRISTMAS WE CELEBRATE THE BIRTH OF JESUS. Let's think about the very first people who heard that Jesus had been born. *(Show the picture of the shepherds out in the fields.)* Who are these people? *(Shepherds.)* What do shepherds do? *(Take care of sheep.)*

Imagine that you're a shepherd out in the fields with your sheep a long, long time ago the night that Jesus was born, before the angels came. What do you hear? see? smell? *(Responses.)* How do you feel? *(Peaceful, thoughtful, watchful.)* How would you feel if all of a sudden an army of angels appeared? *(Startled, surprised, afraid.)* The Gospel story tells us that the shepherds were terrified.

But the angel of the Lord told them, "Do not be afraid; for see—I am bringing you good news." What was that good news? *(Responses.)* Yes, Jesus had been born. The shepherds would find a baby wrapped in bands of cloth and lying in a manger. What happened after the angels left? *(Responses.)* Yes, the shepherds went to Bethlehem and found Mary, Joseph, and baby Jesus. *(Show the picture of the shepherds with baby Jesus.)* How do you think the shepherds felt? *(Thankful, joyful, happy.)*

God could have sent the angels to tell the good news to the priests, or the king, or the rich merchants. Instead, God sent the angels to ordinary shepherds. Why do you think God did that? *(Responses.)* Yes, God sent Jesus for everyone, not just for rich or famous people. By sending the angels to the shepherds, God showed that Jesus is God's gift for everyone.

The Bible story tells us that the shepherds returned to their sheep glorifying and praising God. One way we can glorify and praise God is by singing. Let's sing *(name of carol or song)*. *(You might want to invite the congregation to sing with you.)* — **C. S.**

The Gospel: Luke 2:1-20

Focus: The best gift we can give God is ourselves.

Experience: The children will watch as you are wrapped in gift wrap. They will discuss alternative ways that we can give ourselves to God.

Preparation: Bring a large amount of recycled gift wrap or several colored comic sections from the newspaper, transparent tape, recycled bows, and a bag for holding these items. Make a gift tag that says: To God. Arrange with two adults or two older children to wrap and unwrap you.

Our Gift to God

MERRY CHRISTMAS! What are we celebrating today? *(The birth of Jesus.)* Jesus was God's gift to everyone. I've been trying to think of a gift I could give God, and I've finally decided on one. What do you think it is? *(Listen to their responses. If someone says, "You," say, "That's right! I've decided to give God me!" Quite likely they will not guess. Then continue.)* Those are all good ideas, but I've decided on something different. I'm going to give God—me!

Now that you know that I'm the gift, would you help wrap me like a present? *(Give them the bag and take out the supplies. The persons you contacted earlier may come over to help. While they're wrapping you, make comments that go along with what the children are saying.)*

Being wrapped up like a gift isn't as much fun as I thought it would be. I can't move my arms or legs. I can't do much of anything. I really wanted to give myself to God. Is there some other way? *(Responses.)* Maybe instead of wrapping ourselves up like a present, we could do a lot of good things to serve God. We could help others, use our talents for God, pray, praise and thank God, be kind to other people, read or listen to the Bible, and tell others about God.

Those are good ideas, aren't they? But I can't do those things when I'm wrapped. *(Invite the children to unwrap you and put the wrappings in the bag.)*

There, that feels better. I'm glad that people don't have to get all wrapped up to give themselves to God.

Let's pray. God, we want to give ourselves to you. We want to be your children. Thank you for taking us just the way we are. Amen. **— C.S.**

The Gospel: Matthew 2:13-15, 19-23

Focus: God talks to us.

Experience: The children will remember the danger that Herod posed for Jesus and find out how God told Joseph what to do. They will discuss other ways that God talks to us.

Preparation: Bring nativity figures of Mary, Joseph, and Jesus.

Messages from God

I BROUGHT SOME NATIVITY FIGURES WITH ME TODAY. *(Hold up each one individually and invite the children to tell you who they are and a little about each one.)* What other people and animal figures are often also included in a nativity scene? *(Responses.)* If I had all those figures, we could use them to act out the story of Christmas, except for one part. There's always one figure missing, the king of Judea. He ruled over the place where Jesus was born. What was the name of this king? *(Herod. If they don't know, tell them.)*

When King Herod heard that a special baby had been born, he was afraid. Why do you think a king was afraid of a little baby like Jesus? *(Responses; they may not know.)* The Wise Men had called this baby the King of the Jews. King Herod was afraid that this baby would take away his job and become king instead of him. King Herod was so afraid of Jesus that he decided to kill him.

God knew that Jesus was in danger. Today's Gospel reading tells how Jesus escaped from King Herod. Do you know what happened? *(Some may; but fill in whatever is needed.)* God sent an angel to Joseph in a dream. The angel warned Joseph that Herod wanted to kill Jesus. The angel told Joseph to take Mary and Jesus to Egypt and to stay there until they were told to come back.

God sent a message to Joseph in a dream. Sometimes God talks to us in our dreams. What are some other ways God talks to us? *(Through other people, our conscience, the Bible, prayer.)*

Let's pray. Thank you, God, for speaking to us in different ways. Help us to listen for your messages. Amen. **— C. S.**

Second Sunday after Christmas

The Gospel: John 1:1-18

Focus: We learn about God through Jesus.

Experience: The children will learn about someone's favorite relative. They will review what they learned and then explore the idea that we learn about God through Jesus.

Preparation: Invite one of the older children to tell the others about a favorite relative that most or all of the other children have never met. Ask the child to tell about the person's personality, what he or she likes and dislikes, hobbies, interests, professions, and unusual experiences. Invite an older child to read aloud John 1:18a when asked, or be prepared to read it yourself. Mark that verse in a Bible.

Learning about God Through Jesus

TODAY *(name of volunteer)* is going to tell us about a favorite relative. Listen to find out all you can about *(name of volunteer)*'s relative. *(Name of volunteer)*, tell us about your relative. *(You may need to prompt the volunteer by asking questions about the person's likes and dislikes, appearance, hobbies, experiences, and so forth. Thank the volunteer when he or she is finished.)*

Now, I'd like you to raise your hand if you've never met this person that *(name of volunteer)* told us about. *(Ask those students who have their hands raised to tell you something they remember about the relative. After nearly everything about the relative has been repeated, continue the discussion.)*

You've told me all sorts of things about *(name of volunteer)*'s relative. Are you sure you've never met this person? *(Responses.)* It sounds like you know this person pretty well.

Let's listen to something that we heard in the Gospel reading. *(Have the reader, chosen ahead of time, read John 1:18a. Thank him or her. Otherwise read it yourself.)* What does this verse tell us about God? *(No one has seen God.)* *(Name of first volunteer)* came to help us get to know *(his or her)* relative whom we'd never seen. Who came to teach us about God? *(Jesus.)* How does Jesus help us to know God? *(Responses; they may not know.)* Yes, we can read in the Bible what Jesus said about God. He said God loves each one of us very much. Since Jesus is the Son of God, we learn about God as we get to know Jesus, and we know how much Jesus loves us.

Let's pray. Thank you, Jesus, for teaching us about God. Amen.
— C. S.

The Epiphany of Our Lord

The Gospel: Matthew 2:1-12

Focus: As the Magi gave of their treasures to Jesus, so children can give of their love to Jesus.

Experience: The children will experience the value of treasures and the joy of giving from those treasures.

Preparation: Find a treasure chest, a large decorated box, or some substitute for a treasure chest. The chest should be large enough to hold big items such as teddy bears, but not so large that a watch might seem to get lost in it. If no chest is available, you can create an imaginary one with your hands since the children will be putting imaginary items into it.

Treasure Chests

DO YOU KNOW WHAT A TREASURE IS? *(Encourage responses. Something you find at the bottom of the sea. Something you find in a cave. Your grandmother may have a treasure chest in the attic with clothes and jewelry and things.)* A treasure can be something old or something that has been hidden for a long time. A treasure can also be something that costs a lot like a diamond ring. A treasure is something that you might hide in a hole in the wall or under your mattress, or put in the bank to keep safe.

I brought a treasure chest with me. *(Show treasure chest or shape one with your hands.)* If you had a treasure chest like this, what would you put in it for safekeeping? *(A silver dollar, a picture of grandmother, your teddy bear, your father's watch, the Bible.)* These are all things that we want to keep safe, because they are treasures that we don't want to lose.

The Bible says that when people came to see the baby Jesus, they brought him gifts. It says that the Wise Men, who made a long trip to find Jesus by following a bright star, opened their treasure chests and gave him very valuable gifts. They gave Jesus things that they might have wanted to keep for themselves: gold, frankincense, and myrrh. Frankincense and myrrh were like perfumes, very expensive, and often used in worship. You know what gold is—that is really expensive!

Why do you think they gave treasures to Jesus? *(They loved him. He was the Son of God. He was a baby.)*

If you found baby Jesus today lying in a manger, are there any gifts that you would give him from your treasures? *(Let the children answer. If no answers are given, tell the children that they might want to think about it for a while.)*

Jesus isn't a baby in a manger anymore, so we can't give him gifts the way the Wise Men did, but we can give him our love. And we can give gifts to others, to members of our family, to our friends, and to the poor. When we give gifts to others, we are showing love, and we are giving Jesus our love.

Let's say a prayer to Jesus.

Jesus, thank you for coming into our hearts. Lots of love is there for you, Jesus. May you feel that love when we give gifts from our treasures to others. Amen. **—W.Y.**

The Baptism of Our Lord,
First Sunday after the Epiphany

JAN. 7, 1996   JAN. 10, 1999   JAN. 13, 2002

The Gospel: Matthew 3:13-17

Focus: God showed pleasure with Jesus at his baptism and shows pleasure with all people through their baptisms.

Experience: The children will learn that God is pleased with them by thinking about (1) the way in which adults show them their pleasure, (2) the way God showed pleasure to Jesus through baptism, and (3) how they can remember that God shows them pleasure each morning when they wash their faces.

Preparation: Practice the imaginary actions of turning on water and washing your face. A basin with water and a towel may be used if the number of children is small.

God's Children Are His Pleasure

HOW DO YOU KNOW WHEN YOUR PARENTS or other adults are pleased with you? What do they do when they like what you are doing? *(They smile at me. They clap when we sing for them. They say, "I love you." My teacher winks at me. They put an arm around me.)* Yes, parents and other adults show us that they are pleased with us by hugging us, by saying words that make us feel good, and by showing us signs of pleasure like smiling at us or clapping when we sing or do something special.

Today we read in the Bible that God showed Jesus that he was pleased with him when Jesus was baptized by John the Baptist. When Jesus was baptized, God showed him that he was very pleased with him by lighting up the heavens very brightly (which was a sure sign!), and by saying to Jesus, "I am pleased with you."

Baptism made Jesus feel so close to God. Later on Jesus told his disciples to baptize all God's children.

Now I want to show you a way that you can feel God's pleasure every morning just as Jesus felt God's pleasure at baptism. When you get up in the morning, you can go into the bathroom and turn on the water. *(Demonstrate with actions.)* After you get the water at the temperature you want it, take some water in your hand like this *(cup your hand and bring it to your face)* and splash it on your face *(demonstrate)* as a sign that God is pleased with you and loves you. Then say to yourself: "God is pleased with me today. God loves me."

Let's practice together. Turn on the water. *(Show action.)* Get the temperature just right. Make a cup with your hands and catch some water. *(Show action.)* Splash water on your face. *(Show action.)* Now say what I say: "God is pleased with me today. God loves me." *(God is pleased with me today. God loves me.)* "That's good." *(That's good.)* "Amen." *(Amen.)* **—W.Y.**

The Gospel: John 1:29-41

Focus: Jesus took away the sin of the world.

Experience: The children will experience the relief of having the effects of sin wiped away like words being wiped clean from a magic slate.

Preparation: Have a magic slate and writing instrument ready.

Wipe It Clean

ARE THERE THINGS THAT YOU SAY OR DO that you wish you could erase from your mind and forget? What might they be? *(Write responses on the magic slate. You may have to give examples. Mean words. Hitting. Bad words. Biting. Lies.)*

How do you feel about things you have said or done that you wish you had not said or done? *(Lousy. Ashamed. Guilty.)*

When I was a child, mothers and fathers used to say, "We are going to wipe the slate clean." A slate is like a chalkboard. That always made us kids feel good because it meant they were going to erase all the bad things we did. We wouldn't be in trouble any more. Sometimes a teacher would say it at the end of a day of arguing and fighting. "We are going to wipe the slate clean and start over tomorrow." It would be just like pulling up this sheet and erasing these words.

Do you think that by the next day everybody had forgotten what happened the day before? Some did. Some didn't. It's hard to wipe anger and hatred and meanness off the brain and sweep them out of the heart, but it is worth trying.

Today the Bible tells us that Jesus came and took all our sins away. Sins are all the bad things that we and other people do and think and feel. Where sin had been before, Jesus put love. People said that Jesus was the Lamb of God that takes away the sin of the world, and he took each of our sins away, too.

Tell me, why did he take our sins away and forgive us? *(He knew they were hurting us. Other responses.)* And how does Jesus feel about each one of us, you and you and you *(point to the children)* and me? *(He loves us!)* Yes, he does love us! Let's say it together, "Jesus loves us." *(Jesus loves us.)* **—W.Y.**

31

Third Sunday after the Epiphany

The Gospel: Matthew 4:12-23

Focus: Jesus called four fishermen to be his disciples.

Experience: The children will share what they want to be when they grow up and also think about what they want to do in the church when they grow up. In both they will be workers for Jesus.

Preparation: Identify some church members whose secular work and congregational work you can describe. Alert them to be prepared to stand when you talk about them.

Jesus Calls Us

GIRLS AND BOYS, DO YOU EVER THINK ABOUT what you want to do when you grow up? *(Encourage responses such as teacher, bus driver, store manager, lawyer, astronaut, zookeeper, nurse, engineer, and so forth. Be sure to avoid sexual stereotyping.)* There are so many different jobs you could do that you might wonder how you will ever choose one. Your mind might change several times, but with your parents' help, the help of others, and God's help, you will some day be able to do what you want to do.

We read today in the Bible about four people who grew up to be fishermen. Their names were Peter, Andrew, James, and John. They probably always wanted to be fishermen, and fishermen they became! Every day they went out in their boats if the weather was not too bad, and they fished with big nets. Most of what they caught they sold so that they could buy food, clothing, and what was needed for their families. Fishing was hot, hard work. Sometimes it could be cold, hard work. It could be dangerous work, too, because storms might come up suddenly that could make their boats tip over.

One day Jesus came by and saw them fishing. He called them to shore and said to them, "Come, follow me, and I will make you fishers of people." Instead of only fishing for fish, Jesus told them that they could help him find people for his church. So they dropped their nets and went with him. From now on they would not only be fishermen, they would be disciples of Jesus, too.

When you grow up, you might become a teacher or bricklayer or truck driver or zookeeper or lawyer, and you will also be a worker for Jesus.

(Adjust the following for the people you will be identifying. Be sure to emphasize that they are working for Jesus in their secular occupations as well as in their church activities.) You can be an electrician and work for Jesus, just like Mr.

McCoy standing over there. Or you may become a lawyer like Mrs. Schaeffer, who works for Jesus, too, not only by being a lawyer but also by teaching Sunday school. Mrs. Keyes over there is a fifth-grade teacher. She also prepares the Holy Communion for us at church. She is a worker for Jesus in school and here. Mrs. Leighty once worked in a bank and now she is a homemaker. Organizing the rummage sale and teaching Bible school are just a few things that Mrs. Leighty has done in our church. Mr. Maham operates a store in the mall where you can buy jeans and shirts and jackets. On his day off, which is usually Wednesday, he comes to church and fixes things and changes our narthex sign. Mr. Weitendorf in the back row used to climb telephone poles until they made him a supervisor at the telephone company. He is retired now. All his life he has been a worker for Jesus, too, in his job and here at church. One kind thing he does is to make coffee for the Sunday school teachers and staff every Sunday.

You see, boys and girls, it is important to think about what you want to be when you grow up, what work you will do in the world and what work you will do in the church. In both you will be working for Jesus.

Let's pray together. God, thank you for the ideas you give us about what we can do when we grow up. Thank you for the people in our church who go to work every day and work in our church every week. Thank you that when we grow up, we can be workers for Jesus, too. Amen. **—W.Y.**

Fourth Sunday after the Epiphany

The Gospel: Matthew 5:1-12

Focus: All life is a blessing given by God.

Experience: Through the use of a litany, the children will learn to appreciate the common things of life as blessings.

Life Is a Blessing

GOOD MORNING, GIRLS AND BOYS! This is such a wonderful day. I always look forward to Sunday mornings, and especially to being with you and talking with you about God and life and love. Do you know how I would describe it? I would say, "It is a blessing to be with you." Do you understand what I mean when I say it is a blessing to be with you? *(Responses. It's good. It makes you happy. It is special. You like us.)*

The Gospel lesson in the Bible today uses the word "blessed," and I wonder how often you have heard the words "blessed" or "blessing" used. A blessing is what someone gives you when they say "God bless you!" When have you heard someone say "God bless you?" *(Responses. When you sneeze. When they say goodbye.)* When I sneeze and someone says "God bless you," I feel like that person has just thrown a blanket of love over me to make me feel cozy and to help me stop tingling all over from the sneeze. A blessing is like a blanket of love.

A wise man once said, "Just to *be* is a blessing."* Can you say that for me? *(Just to* be *is a blessing.)*

So if I said: just to be alive, to breathe, to smell, to taste, to hear, to talk is a blessing, do you know what you could say? Just to *be* is a blessing. *(The children repeat it.)* Just to drink some milk, some juice, or soda pop, to eat a whole meal, even veggies, is a blessing. What do you say? *(Just to* be *is a blessing.)*

Maybe you have some ideas about what blessings are to you. What is a blessing to you? What are some things you really enjoy? *(To pet my dog. To get hugs. To play video games.)* These things are blessings. What do you say, congregation? *(Just to* be *is a blessing.)*

What other blessings, good things, can you think of? *(To sleep at grandma's. To sing "Jesus Loves Me." To play.)* What do we say to that? *(Just to* be *is a blessing.)*

---

* Heschel, Abraham Joshua. *I Asked for Wonder: A Spiritual Anthology.* Ed. Samuel H. Dresner. (New York: Crossroad, 1985).

I have some ideas, too. Just to make a friend, please a teacher, forgive a meanie, or help a neighbor is a blessing. What do you say? *(Just to* be *is a blessing.)*

And just to love as Jesus loves, just to be like Jesus is a blessing, and just to live with Jesus some day will be a real blessing. What do you say? *(Just to* be *is a blessing.)*

If I say, "God bless you," do you know what I mean? I think that you do, because "just to *be* is a blessing." God bless you. **—W.Y.**

The Gospel: Matthew 5:13-20

Focus: Jesus said that we are the salt of the earth.

Experience: The children will learn that the world needs them and their love in the way that salt is needed for life.

Preparation: Bring a large salt block for demonstration (or a box of salt) and enough small salt pellets (or envelopes of salt) to give one to each child.

You Are the Salt of the Earth

DO YOU KNOW WHAT THIS IS THAT I HOLD IN MY HANDS? *(Hold up the salt block [or box of salt]. Allow responses.)* It looks like a big cake of soap, but it is a salt block. *(If you brought a box of salt, mention that salt can be pressed together into a block for animals to lick on.)* People put salt blocks out to attract deer, because deer need salt to live.

All animals, including human beings, need salt in their diet in order to live. Animals that eat meat, like tigers, rattlesnakes, and dogs don't need a salt block because they get enough salt from the meat they eat. We get enough salt from the meat that we eat and from the food that comes in cans or packages, but animals that eat only grass and seeds and plants need extra salt. A farmer once told me that he has seen horses lick the ground in order to get salt out of the earth.

In Jesus' time salt was also needed to keep food from spoiling because they did not have refrigerators. Sometimes there wasn't always enough salt to go around, and that could be a problem.

Today we read in the Bible that Jesus said, "You are the salt of the earth." The love that you share is as important to people as salt is for our bodies. Love is like salt when you share it. Salt is important, love is important. The world needs people who love other people, who don't cheat or steal or hate, and who are kind and care and share and forgive.

To help you to remember that you are the salt of the earth, that your love is good and is important, I am going to give you a salt pellet like the ones that are sometimes put in rabbit cages *(or envelopes of salt)*. And remember, when you hear that you are the salt of the earth, that means you can help people with one of their real needs—you can *love* them. **—W.Y.**

FEB. 11, 1996

The Gospel: Matthew 5:20-37

Focus: Jesus commanded us to transcend anger by seeking reconciliation and peace with our neighbors.

Experience: Children will think about the things that they can do to make anger go away.

Preparation: Prepare a poster with the motto, "Don't get mad; get smart" and the four actions suggested in this sermon: ask for time out, go somewhere to be alone, talk about it, and make peace. Drawings may supplement the words.

Don't Get Mad; Get Smart

WE KNOW THAT THE THINGS WE DO that hurt others make us feel ashamed and guilty, and we are thankful that Jesus takes sin away and replaces it with love. Many of the things people do that are called sins happen when people are angry. Sometimes we can't help getting angry, but there are things we can do to keep things from getting worse.

Andrew Young, a former ambassador to the United Nations, says that his father used to say to him, "Don't get mad. Get smart!"* So let's think about how we can get smart instead of getting mad.

First let's talk about the times when we might get angry. When do children get angry? (Responses. *When somebody keeps something instead of sharing, or tells a lie, or breaks something of mine, or takes something that belongs to me, or does something that is unfair.*)

Let's see what we can do when these things happen and we get angry. That way we will show others that we are smart, too. (*Show poster.*) You can't all read yet so I will read it to you.

1. We can *ask for time out.* We can say, "Holy Smoke! I'm getting hot. I need a time out." We can cool down by drinking ice water or soda pop.

2. We can *go somewhere to be alone.* One mother went into a closet one day to get away from an argument instead of sending her kids to their bedrooms. It surprised the kids! Kids can go somewhere to be alone, too.

3. We can *talk about it.* After we have cooled off, we can say, "I want to talk, because I was getting angry."

---

* Young, Andrew. *A Way Out of No Way.* (Nashville: Thomas Nelson Publishers, 1994).

4. We can *make peace* by shaking hands, giving a gift, or saying something nice.

Remember next time that you start to get angry, say to yourself, "Don't get mad. Get smart." **— W.Y.**

The Gospel: Matthew 5:38-48

Focus: Jesus taught us to "turn the other cheek."

Experience: The children will learn that "getting even" is really impossible and that acts of kindness are more effective.

The Sin of Getting Even

WE ARE TALKING ABOUT SIN AGAIN TODAY. Sin is what we do that hurts others and makes us feel ashamed and guilty. Today we read in the Bible that "getting even" is a sin. Did you know that "getting even" is a sin?

Let's see if we can figure out why "getting even" is a sin. Imagine that you just called me a cabbage head. You didn't really mean to hurt me, but in your excitement or your frustration, you called me a cabbage head. I don't like it that you called me a cabbage head, so I decide to get even. So I call you a stupid jerk. Would that make us even? *(Responses.)* Would it stop us from calling each other names? Probably not.

If somebody pushes you in a line, and you push that person back, the other person will probably not think that you got even. Instead the person you pushed will get upset and think that you pushed too hard or that you started it all, and probably push you harder or even hit you. Things can only get worse when we try to get even.

So the Bible says that getting even is a sin. The Bible says it is a sin because it is impossible to get even. Things just get worse. We should quit trying to get even.

Jesus had a better idea. Jesus said that when somebody does something to hurt you or make you upset, try doing something kind to that person in return. Treat meanness with kindness, says Jesus. It won't always be easy. So when someone calls me a cabbage head, what could I do that wouldn't get me into trouble? *(Responses.)* Sometimes we can't think of anything kind to do, but doing nothing might be better than doing something. So I might just ignore the person. Doing nothing might be a kind thing to do.

Jesus calls it "turning the other cheek." Jesus will help us to figure out what to do. When something happens and we are tempted to get even, we can ask him for help to figure out what to do. Jesus is always with us. **—W.Y.**

The Gospel: Matthew 6:24-34

Focus: Jesus tells us not to be anxious about the future because our future is in God's hands.

Experience: The children will explore their own worries and learn to pray about their worries with the help of a worry stone.

Preparation: Bring small stones, perhaps polished stones, at least one inch in diameter to give to each child to take and carry as a worry stone.

Worry Free

DO YOU EVER WORRY? What do you worry about? *(Responses. I will get lost. I will get hurt. Kids will make fun of me. My mommy or daddy will get sick.)*

Today we read in the Bible that Jesus said we need not worry because God will take care of us. God says we should be free as birds, who do not worry about what they will eat tomorrow or what they should wear today. Birds don't worry, but we humans do worry because our brains are bigger than bird brains, and we have much more on our minds.

Sometimes we worry about little things. We worry about who is going to be first in line for ice cream at the church potluck, but we shouldn't worry about that because everybody gets ice cream anyway. There is always enough for everybody. We may worry whose team we are going to play with on the playground, but we shouldn't worry about that, because it is only a game.

Other worries are big worries. We worry about lightning striking our house, which it probably won't. We worry about the cat dying if it gets sick, which it might or might not. Will my parents find me after Sunday school, we worry, even though they always do. We worry about being hurt and being forgotten and losing a friend and things like that. These are big worries.

So for the big worries, I have something for you. I have brought a worry stone for each of you. This is what you do. When you feel a big worry coming on, get your stone, and put it in your pocket or under your pillow or take it in your hand and just start rubbing it with worry. You can also say a prayer to Jesus while you are rubbing your worry away.

So now that everyone has a worry stone, let's practice. First we need to worry. Let's worry that we will lose our worry stone! So start rubbing the stone with worry *(demonstrate)*, and say after me, "Jesus, help me *(Jesus, help me)* rub my worry away *(rub my worry away)*. Thank you. *(Thank you.)* Amen. *(Amen.)*" **—W.Y.**

The Transfiguration of Our Lord,
Last Sunday after the Epiphany

The Gospel: Matthew 17:1-9

Focus: Jesus was transfigured in light before Peter and James and John, and these words were heard: "This is my Son, the Beloved, with whom I am well pleased. Listen to him."

Experience: The children will experience the effect that light has on a person when a flashlight is shined on that person. They will hear that Jesus can help them, too, as they stand in the light of Christ.

Preparation: Ask the ushers to dim the lights in the sanctuary soon after the children come forward. Bring a large flashlight with fresh batteries in it.

Transformed by the Light of Christ

BOYS AND GIRLS, DO YOU KNOW WHERE LIGHT COMES FROM? *(Responses. The sun, the moon, light bulbs, street lights, and so forth.)* Some light comes directly from the sun or from a light bulb that runs on electricity. Some light is reflected light, like the moon. The moon does not have its own light. It sends us light by reflecting the sun's light to us just as a mirror might reflect light to us. Direct light comes from the sun and light bulbs, but the light that comes from a mirror or the moon is reflected light.

(Alert ushers to shut off the lights.) It's darker now, isn't it? Watch what happens when I shine this flashlight across the congregation. *(Shine flashlight in congregation and move it like a spotlight.)* As the light falls on different people, they shine with reflected light. When I take the flashlight away *(turn flashlight toward the floor)*, you can hardly tell who they are because of all the shadows of darkness.

If I take this flashlight and shine it on Mr. Randall right there *(shine flashlight on a worshiper)*, he lights up, doesn't he? If I take it away, he doesn't shine anymore. People don't shine with their own light. *(Turn flashlight away toward the floor.)* They can only reflect light.

Today we read in the Bible that Jesus went up on a mountain, and while he was there, he was *transfigured* by a great flash of light. His face got really bright and his clothes looked as if they were pure white. Jesus shone brightly with light, because he stood in the light of God on that mountain.

So, too, when we pray to Jesus and hear stories about him from the Bible, it is as though we are standing in Jesus' light. Young Reid over here is not giving off much light, but if I shine the flashlight on him *(shine flashlight toward a youth)*, he lights up. And if I shine this flashlight on any of you, you light up, too. *(Turn flashlight on children.)*

Jesus helps us to do good deeds and kind acts. Then we, too, are reflecting his light to others. We are not the light, but we can stand in Jesus' light and give light to others by the kind of lives we lead. **—W.Y.**

The Gospel: Matthew 4:1-11

Focus: We need food for our bodies and food for our faith.

Experience: You and the children will talk together about the fact that we need more than just one kind of food to be healthy.

Preparation: Bring pictures from magazines of different types of food, both healthy and snack foods.

What Do You Need?

TODAY I BROUGHT SOMETHING WITH ME. *(Hold up one of the pictures.)* Do you know what this is? *(Ask them to name the food.)* That's right. *(Continue to show the pictures, asking them to name the foods.)* That's right. God has created many types of foods for us to eat.

What if I said this to you? "You may choose any of these foods but from then on that's the only kind of food you can eat for the rest of your life." Would you be very happy about that? *(No.)* Would that be very healthy for you? *(No.)* No, it wouldn't be. In order to be healthy, we need to eat a balanced diet from a variety of food groups.

We need to eat a variety of foods, don't we? We can't just eat snacks. We can eat spaghetti, soup, sandwiches, vegetables, fruit, and other good foods. Do you like to eat spaghetti? *(Responses.)* Soup? *(Responses.)* What kinds? *(Responses.)* There are many good foods that our moms and dads help us choose, aren't there?

In order to have healthy bodies we need to eat many kinds of foods. We need food that helps our eyes, muscles, teeth, bones, every part of us. All of these foods are important.

In today's Bible story, Jesus says something interesting. He said, "One does not live by bread alone, but by every word that comes from the mouth of God." Jesus meant that for daily living, food is important, but even though bread and other foods feed our bodies, that's not enough. Our faith needs food too.

What kinds of things do you think can feed your faith in God? What can you do? *(Provide hints as needed. Pray, read the Bible and Bible story books, go to church and Sunday school, sing, talk about God with your parents and others, and so on.)* That's right. Just as different kinds of food feed our bodies and help them to grow, so prayer, worship, and learning about God help to feed

43

our faith in God. Jesus says we need healthy bodies and a growing faith in order to live happy lives.

Let's pray. Thank you, God, for giving us food for our bodies and food for our faith. Help us to learn and grow up in you. Amen. — **L. R.**

The Gospel: John 4:5-26

Focus: By offering the woman "living water," Jesus was trying to help her understand that she had faith needs as well as physical needs.

Experience: You will show the children a picture of an item and ask them whether they would rather have the picture or the actual thing.

Preparation: Clip a picture of candy from a magazine or a Sunday paper ad. Bring pieces of candy for all the children as well as some sugar-free candy or fruit. Put them in a large grocery bag so the children cannot see them.

What Jesus Gives Is Real

I HAVE SOMETHING SPECIAL FOR YOU TODAY. I was thinking it would be nice to have a little treat together. What do you think about that? *(Responses.)* Would you like some candy? I have some right inside this bag. *(Responses.)* Great! I was hoping you'd be interested.

(Reach into the bag as though you intend to pull out some candy. Then pause.) What kinds of candy do you like? *(Responses. Look through your bag and talk to them about how you hope they'll enjoy the candy you have. Then bring out the picture of the candy.)* Here you go! I hope you will enjoy this candy! *(Pause for comments. If there are none, prompt them by saying things like, "Aren't you glad I brought this candy for you?")* You're right. A picture of candy isn't the same as real candy, is it?

In today's Bible story, Jesus talked with a woman at a well. The story in the Bible isn't about candy. It's about water. The woman went to the well to get water for drinking and cooking. Jesus asked her if she would give him a drink. Jesus told her that even though real water is nice, just like this picture of candy is nice, her faith needed a different kind of water—"living water."

We could say that "living water" can mean God's Word, the Bible, or God's Spirit. We all need living water to learn about God and to grow in faith. That's what we do each time we come to church. We receive living water from God that will help us to know God better and better.

I was only teasing you earlier when I offered you candy and only gave you a picture, wasn't I? I will give you some candy later. *(Show them what you brought along.)* I also have some fruit and sugar-free candy. At the end of the worship service, I will stand by the front door *(or wherever)* and give each of you a treat if your parents don't mind.

The Bible tells us that God is a good giver. God gives us what we need. For our bodies, God gives food and water and homes and people to help and care for us. For our faith, God gives living water like the Bible, the love of other Christians, and joy and peace in our hearts.

Let's pray. Thank you, God, for giving us everything we need: things for our bodies and living water for our faith. Amen. **— L. R.**

The Gospel: John 9:1-41

Focus: We have many names for Jesus and many ways of talking and thinking about him. Each of us needs to know Jesus in order to tell others about him.

Experience: The children will look around the worship area and talk about things that remind them of Jesus.

Preparation: If you wish, you may bring in artwork or symbols to help the children talk about Jesus as the Good Shepherd, teacher, friend, Prince of Peace, Lamb of God, and so on.

What Do You Say about Him?

TODAY THE GOSPEL STORY IS ABOUT a blind man who was healed by Jesus. The people who knew the blind man were amazed because they didn't expect that the man would ever be able to see again. They couldn't believe it!

They asked the blind man, "What do you have to say about Jesus? Who do you think he is?"

The blind man hadn't known Jesus very long, but he answered, "He is a prophet." Do you know what a prophet is? *(The children may have heard the word but most will not know. The main definition is that a prophet is one who speaks God's Word.)* Jesus was a prophet. He spoke God's Word to the people.

Jesus has many other names too. If someone asked you, "Who is Jesus?" what would you tell them? *(Affirm their responses and continue the discussion, prompting them as needed.)*

Look around the worship area. Is there anything here that reminds you of Jesus? *(Responses. You may wish to point to some things; for instance, the cross reminds us that Jesus is our Savior. The candles can remind us that Jesus is the light of the world. You may call attention to paintings, stained glass, sculpture, paraments, pictures you have brought along, and so on, emphasizing how each tells something about Jesus—Good Shepherd, teacher, friend, Prince of Peace, Lamb of God, and so forth.)*

That's right. All of these things help us to think about Jesus and learn to know him better. And when we learn about Jesus, we can know what to answer when someone asks us, "Who is Jesus?" What are some of the answers you would give if someone asks you who Jesus is? *(Responses. Help them say some of the names or descriptions that have been mentioned.)* Yes, Jesus is the

Son of God, Jesus is our Savior, Jesus is our friend, and Jesus is with us always.

Let's pray. Thank you, Jesus, for coming to earth so that we can know you. Help us to know you better each day. Thank you for being our friend. Amen.

— L. R.

The Gospel: Matthew 20:17-28

Focus: The way Jesus defined greatness is different from the way most people define it.

Experience: You will talk with the children about why we call some people great and about how Jesus' ideas of greatness are different from what many people think.

The Wish to Be Great

WHEN WE WATCH TV OR LISTEN TO THE RADIO or look at magazines, we find out about people who are famous. What are some of them famous for? *(Responses. Being TV or movie stars, being good in sports, making a lot of money.)* Why is *(name a TV or movie star)* famous? *(Responses. He or she acts well, sings well, is good looking.)* Why is *(name a well-known political figure such as the president)* famous? *(He is our president; other responses.)*Why is *(name a cartoon figure)* famous? *(Responses.)* And *(name of cartoon figure)* isn't even a real person! Why is *(name sports figures, singers, others, as time allows)* famous? *(Responses.)*

So there are many people who are famous. Sometimes we use the word *great* to describe famous people. Some may say *(the president, a sports personality, other people named before)* are great. Some may even call a rough person great because he can beat up on a lot of people. So people have all kinds of ideas about what it means to be great.

From the Gospel reading today, we find out what Jesus said about greatness. He said that those who wish to be great need to be like servants; they need to be willing to love and help other people. So in Jesus' eyes, which of these people would be really great: first, people who earn lots of money but spend most of it on themselves, or second, people who do kind and helpful things for others every day? *(Responses.)* Yes, kind people show true greatness.

Jesus himself was very kind and loving, and we call him great. What did Jesus do that was kind and loving? *(Responses. Provide clues if needed; he healed people, fed them, talked with them, accepted them, and finally died on a cross to save us all from our sins.)* As followers of Jesus, we are to be kind to people, too. That's the best kind of greatness.

Let's pray. Thank you, Jesus, for showing us that being kind, helpful, and loving are more important than having the world think we are famous. Amen. **— L. R.**

Fifth Sunday in Lent

The Gospel: John 11:1-53

Focus: Jesus loved his friends. Jesus loves us.

Experience: You will talk with the children about how friends feel about each another and compare their responses to how Jesus felt about Lazarus.

Jesus Is Our Friend

TODAY'S GOSPEL STORY IS ABOUT A MAN named Lazarus. Lazarus was one of Jesus' friends. Jesus had some good friends. What do you think they did together? *(Responses. They talked, ate, walked, worked, laughed. You could prompt them by asking, "Do you think they talked? Walked?" And so on.)*

What kinds of things do you do with your friends? *(Responses. Make connections between the things Jesus did with his friends.)* It sounds as if you do some of the same things with your friends that Jesus did with his!

When something great happens to one of your friends, how do you feel? *(Happy.)* Yes, and isn't that a good feeling? When something bad happens to one of your friends, how do you feel? *(Sad.)* That's right. It's hard when bad things happen to our friends. We feel bad too.

Something bad happened to Jesus' friend Lazarus. He got very sick. Lazarus's two sisters sent a message to Jesus and asked him to come and visit their brother. They believed that Jesus would be able to help their brother.

Jesus said he would come, but it took him several days to get there, and while he was traveling, Lazarus died. All of Lazarus's friends and family were very sad. When Jesus got there and heard the news, he was very sad and began to cry. And do you know what everyone said? They said, "See how he loved him!" They could tell that Jesus loved Lazarus. Jesus was Lazarus's friend.

And Jesus is our friend too. Does that mean that when we're happy, Jesus is happy? *(Yes.)* And when we're sad, Jesus is sad? *(Yes.)* That's right. Jesus is our friend. He cares about how we feel. When you have a friend or someone in your family that you care about, how can you show them that you care? *(Smiles, kind words, hugs.)* When you go back to your places, look for someone you care about and tell them or show them how you feel. Then you can tell them that you're their friend, and Jesus is too.

Let's pray. Thank you, Jesus, for being our friend. Help us to be a friend to others, too. Amen. **— L. R.**

Sunday of the Passion,
Palm Sunday

The Gospel: Matthew 26:1—27:66

Focus: Jesus ate the Passover meal with his disciples and promised that, whenever they ate the bread in that way, Jesus would be with them.

Experience: You will retell the story of the Last Supper. If appropriate to church practice, you and the children could share some bread together, pointing out that some of the words spoken during Holy Communion are from the Gospel reading from Matthew.

Preparation: Bring a small loaf of bread to share together. Have it in a bag so the children cannot see it.

Eat This Bread

TODAY'S BIBLE READING IS A LONG, LONG STORY about some of the things that happened on the night before Jesus died. He was together with his disciples and they ate a meal together. One of the things they ate was made out of flour, formed into loaves or round shapes, and baked in an oven. Do you know what that food was? *(Responses.)* That's right. Bread.

While they were eating, Jesus picked up some bread. *(Show them the bread you brought along.)* Would you like to taste some of the bread? *(Break up the bread and share it among the children who would like a piece.)* Jesus said something important to his disciples when he gave them the bread. He said, "Take, eat; this is my body." He meant that whenever the disciples gathered and shared bread together this way, they should remember Jesus loved them and would always be with them.

And do you know what? We still say those same words here in church. Every time we celebrate Holy Communion, we tell people, "This is the body of Christ, given for you." *(You may need to modify this statement according to your church's practice.)* When we say that, we remember that Jesus died for us. We remember that he loves us and promises to be with us always.

(Depending on your church practices, modify the following.) When you are older, you too will receive bread during Holy Communion. Until that time, remember that Jesus loves you always.

Let's pray. Thank you, Jesus, for your promise to be with us always. Amen.

— L. R.

The Resurrection of Our Lord,
Easter Day

The Gospel: John 20:1-9 or Matthew 28:1-10

Focus: Easter is part of a year-long cycle that tells the story of Jesus' birth, life, death, and resurrection.

Experience: You and the children will talk about how the colors of jelly beans can remind them of the story of Jesus' birth, life, death, and resurrection.

Preparation: Bring a basket or container of jelly beans. It would be best if the jelly bean mixture had the following colors: blue, white, purple, black, red, and green. But if all those colors are not available, that's fine, too. Think about how your church uses color during different seasons of the church year, and speak about these connections as you talk about the colored jelly beans. Adapt the comments as needed.

Telling Jesus' Story

TODAY IS A VERY SPECIAL DAY, ISN'T IT? What is this day called? *(Easter.)* What happened to Jesus on this day? *(Jesus rose from the dead.)* That's right! And we are very happy!

Did any of you find an Easter basket or candy at your house? *(Responses.)* Easter baskets don't have anything to do with the story of Jesus. Easter baskets are just for fun. But I noticed something about my Easter basket. It was filled with all sorts of little things like these. *(Hold up a jelly bean.)* What are these things? *(Jelly beans.)* Yes, and look at all of the pretty colors. All of these colors remind me about Jesus, and they help tell his story. Here, let me tell you about it. *(If your church uses colored banners, paraments, or candles during the church year, you may draw attention to them and remind the children that the colors of these pieces of fabric change throughout the year.)*

(Hold up a blue jelly bean.) Look at this blue jelly bean. Our church uses blue during the season of Advent—the beginning of the story of Jesus—when we wait for his coming to earth as a baby and look forward to his second coming. *(If this—or any other—color is not available, simply say, "There are no blue jelly beans, but the color blue reminds me of the season of Advent.")*

Look! Here's a white jelly bean! *(Hold it up.)* The color white is used at Christmas and Epiphany to celebrate Jesus' birth. Jesus is God's Son—a light to the nations.

And here is a purple one. *(Hold it up.)* Purple reminds us of Jesus the king and we have just seen it in church during Lent—preparing for Jesus' suffering and death.

A black jelly bean! *(Hold it up.)* Black is the color we used on Good Friday. It reminds us that Jesus died on the cross, and that Jesus loves us.

Look, another white one! *(Hold it up.)* White reminds us of Jesus' birth, but it also reminds us of Easter when he rose again—and that's today, right? *(Responses.)*

Ah, my favorite, red! *(Hold it up.)* Red reminds me of the tongues of fire on Pentecost—the beginning of the church.

And finally, the color green. *(Hold it up.)* Who can guess what green is for? *(Responses. You can prompt them by asking, "What kinds of things are green?" and by encouraging them to make connections between green and growing things.)* That's right. Green reminds us of the long season of Pentecost during the summer. In Pentecost we learn what Jesus teaches and we grow in faith.

Well, that's a long story to remember. But next time you look at a jelly bean, remember that Jesus was born, lived, died, and was raised from the dead and that he loves you. You are special to Jesus, and he will always love you the whole year through.

If you would like some jelly beans, meet me at the front door *(or wherever)* after the service and I'll give you each a little bag of jelly beans. Have a wonderful Easter!

Let's pray. Dear Jesus, today we are celebrating! We are happy to be together, and we are happy that you rose from the dead. Thank you for Easter, and thank you for being with us always. Amen. **— L. R.**

Second Sunday of Easter

The Gospel: John 20:19-31

Focus: Jesus' followers wrote down the information about him that we find in Scripture so that we might believe in him as our Lord and Savior and, by believing, have life in his name.

Experience: The children will learn that people have many different purposes for writing words down. In looking at a number of examples of the written word, you and the children will help determine the purpose for them being written. Finally you will focus on the purpose that Jesus' followers had for their writing.

Preparation: Bring a familiar children's book, an advertisement from a magazine, a schoolbook, and the Bible.

That You May Believe

GOD HAS BLESSED US WITH a number of different ways to communicate, to share information with one another. One of those ways, which we use quite often, is by writing things down for others to read. This morning we are going to look at some different kinds of writing and talk about the reasons why we think they were written.

(*Hold up the children's book.*) Who can tell me what this is? (*Responses.*) That's right, this is a storybook. Why do you suppose the author of this book wrote it? (*Responses.*) The author's purpose for writing it was to entertain those who read it. We all enjoy reading stories like this; it's fun to do.

(*Hold up the magazine advertisement.*) Who knows what we call this type of writing? (*Responses.*) Very good! We call this an advertisement or an ad. What does the person who wrote this advertisement hope we will want to do after reading it? (*Responses.*) Yes, the ad writer hopes that we will want to buy what is talked about in the advertisement.

(*Hold up the schoolbook.*) Here is another book, different from the story-book we looked at earlier. What kind of book is it? (*Responses.*) That's right, this is a book used in school. It is about (*name the subject: math, history, and so on*). What does the author of this book want the child who uses it to do? (*Responses.*) Yes, the author wants the child who uses it to learn what is taught in the book.

(*Now hold up the Bible.*) What do we call this book? (*Responses*) Yes, this is the Bible, God's Word for his people. Like all of the other types of writing we looked at this morning, the people who wrote the Bible had a purpose for writing, too. Our Gospel writer for this morning tells us why he and the other followers of Jesus wrote what they wrote. He said, "I wrote these things about Jesus so that you may believe that he is the Christ, the Son of God, and that by believing you may have life in his name." We can be thankful that these Christians wrote about what they saw and believed. We can be thankful that when we read about Jesus, God helps us believe and have the promise of eternal life. **— D. H.**

Third Sunday of Easter

The Gospel: Luke 24:13-35

Focus: God helps us understand the Scriptures so we can know that Jesus Christ is our Lord and Savior.

Experience: The children will identify tools that we use to open various items each day. Ultimately we will help them to understand that it is God who opens the Scripture for us so that we can use and understand it.

Preparation: Bring a key ring (be sure it includes a car key), a can opener, a letter opener, an unopened letter, and the Bible.

Opening Scripture

EVERY DAY WHEN I LEAVE MY HOME I carry this with me *(show them your key ring)*. What are these things called? *(Responses.)* Yes, these are my keys. As I left my house, I reached in my pocket and pulled out this key *(hold up your car key.)* I could not have gotten here without this key. What do you suppose this key opens? *(Responses.)* Yes, I use this key to open my car door so that I can get inside to drive wherever I need to go. All of the other keys on my key ring help me to open other doors that I need to enter: my office, my house, the church, and so forth.

The other day I decided that I was hungry for some soup. I got the can down from the shelf, but I couldn't eat the soup because the can was still closed. What did I need to get the can open? *(Responses.)* That's right, I needed a can opener like this one *(hold up the can opener.)* After using the opener to open the can, I could get to the soup inside, heat it up, eat it, and enjoy it.

I get letters nearly every day at both my office and at home. In order to find out what is inside each envelope I use something to open them. What do you suppose I use? *(Responses.)* Yes, I use this device called a letter opener to neatly open each letter *(demonstrate if you have an unopened envelope with you)*. After using the letter opener, I can remove whatever is inside the envelope and read it.

In our Gospel lesson for today, two men on their way home to a town called Emmaus were having a hard time understanding everything that had just happened. Their friend, Jesus, had been crucified and now they had heard reports that he was alive. They needed someone to help them understand all of this, to unlock the mystery for them. Along came Jesus, but they did not recognize him. He explained for them all that had happened. Jesus was the key for helping them to understand God's plan of salvation for them and for all who believe. When they arrived at their home, they invited Jesus to stay with them. When Jesus sat down at the table, he took bread, gave thanks, broke it and began to give it to them. At once they recognized who he was, but then he disappeared from their sight. They were so excited that they ran back to Jerusalem to tell Jesus' friends, the disciples, that Jesus was alive. Though Jesus was no longer there with them, he had opened the Scriptures for them.

We have the wonderful news of God's love for us in the Bible. When we hear and read God's Word, God helps us so that we, like the men on the road to Emmaus, can see Jesus as our Lord and Savior. Thank you, God, for opening the Scriptures for us!   **— D. H.**

Fourth Sunday of Easter

The Gospel: John 10:1-10

Focus: When Jesus, the Good Shepherd, calls us, we follow because we know his voice and trust him to watch over us and save us.

Experience: The children will, after identifying tools used by others in their occupations, identify the shepherd's most important tool in leading his sheep. That tool is the shepherd's voice.

Preparation: You may wish to bring a hammer, a musical instrument, and an artist's paint brush.

The Voice of the Shepherd

IN THE BIBLE WE HEAR A LOT ABOUT SHEPHERDS. Jesus called himself the Good Shepherd, and all those who followed him would be like his sheep. Just like sheep, without the guidance of our Lord, the Good Shepherd, we would go astray.

This morning we will have you decide what you think the shepherd's most important tool was in getting his sheep to follow him. First, however, let's look at some other jobs and the tools that are important to those doing them.

Does anyone know what we call a person who builds things out of wood? *(Responses.)* That's right, a carpenter. You may recall that Jesus' earthly father, Joseph, was a carpenter. What tools are important for carpenters to have if they wish to build something? *(Responses.)* They need to have a hammer *(show the one you brought)*, a saw, and nails in order to build something from wood.

A person who plays a musical instrument *(show it if you brought one)* is called a musician. Musicians may be very well trained and have tremendous talent, but none of that will mean anything unless they have one very important tool. What do you think that tool is? *(Responses.)* Exactly! Without a musical instrument, the musician cannot make music. That instrument is his or her most important tool.

Sometimes the tool we need to do a job is part of us. In the game of baseball, for example, a pitcher must be able to throw the ball hard. What has to be strong in order for the pitcher to do that? *(Responses.)* Yes, the pitcher must have a strong arm in order to throw well. That arm is that person's most important tool.

We know that shepherds in Biblical times were able to get their sheep to follow them. How did they do that? What was the shepherd's most important tool in getting the sheep to follow him? *(Responses.)* That is correct! The shepherd used his voice to call his sheep. The sheep followed him because they knew and trusted the shepherd's voice. In fact, his was the only voice they would follow.

Jesus, our Good Shepherd, calls us to follow him, too. We hear his voice every Sunday as the pastor shares God's Word with us. Jesus' message to us is that he loves us; so much, in fact, that he was willing to live, die, and rise again for our salvation. Never stop listening to the loving voice of the Savior, and never stop using your voice to tell others about him. **— D. H.**

Fifth Sunday of Easter

The Gospel: John 14:1-12

Focus: The only way to heaven is by trusting in Jesus Christ as our Lord and Savior.

Experience: After talking about the word *way,* the children will share examples of many different ways of doing simple tasks. Then they will hear that there is only one way to heaven: through trusting in Jesus.

Preparation: Bring a pencil or pen (optional: a necktie).

Only One Way

DID YOU KNOW THAT A NAME USED FOR THE CHURCH of Jesus' day was "the way"? People didn't belong to the church, they belonged to "the way." In a little while we'll talk more about that, but first we are going to talk about how we use the word *way* today.

Think of how we use the word *way:* the best way, the right way, the American way. Children will sometimes correct each other when playing a game, "That's not the right *way* to do that!" Have any of you ever said that? *(Responses.)*

There are many ways we can greet another person. We might say, "Hi! Hello! How do you do?" Or we might use some action, like a wave or a hand-shake or a hug.

It's amazing how many different ways there are to tie and wear a necktie. If you look at those wearing ties today, you will see quite a few ways. *(Look out into the congregation; if you brought a tie along, demonstrate a couple of ways.)*

There are quite a few ways for me to go from church to my home. I can *(describe a couple of different routes).* All of them will get me home.

I have always been fascinated by the number of ways people hold a pencil when they write. *(Demonstrate a few or have a child or two show how they hold a pencil.)* All the ways are different, but all of them work.

Now let's get back to our first question: Why did they call the church of Jesus' day "the way"? Our Gospel lesson for today helps us answer it. Jesus told his disciples that he would be going away soon and they were sad. He tried to make them feel better by telling them that after a while they would be with him in heaven. He would provide *the way.* Jesus said these words, "I am *the way,* the truth, and the life; no one comes to the Father but by me."

The disciples knew and loved Jesus. They knew the way to heaven because they believed and trusted in Jesus, and he was the way. Just as Jesus was *the way* for the disciples to get to heaven, so is he *the way* for us to get to heaven. We trust in Jesus as our Lord and Savior, we love him, and we know that he is the way to heaven for us. — **D. H.**

Sixth Sunday of Easter

The Gospel: John 14:15-21

Focus: We obey God as a response to God's love for us.

Experience: The children will begin by defining the word *obey*. They will then look at some examples of obedience and determine which type of obedience God expects from his children.

Preparation: You may wish to ask some youth from your congregation to help present the skit contained in this sermon. Give them their parts to read ahead of time.

If You Love Me

JESUS TALKED A GREAT DEAL ABOUT LOVE IN THE BIBLE. He expected his disciples to love him and also to love one another. He also told his disciples that one way he would know if they loved him would be if they obeyed what he commanded.

Today we want to focus on what it means to obey Christ. Who can tell me what it means to obey someone? *(Responses. To obey someone means to do what they tell you to do, to mind, or to be good.)* Thank you! I think you have a good understanding of what it means to obey.

Now we are going to look at some examples of people being obedient; of people obeying someone. We especially want to look at their reasons for being obedient and to pick out the example that best illustrates the type of obeying that Jesus desires from us.

I have some young friends who are going to help me with this task. Here we have the Moore family. This is Mrs. Moore and her three children, Amy, Brady, and Sue. One day Mrs. Moore had to leave the house to run an important errand. She left some chocolate chip cookies in a container in the kitchen with specific instructions for the children not to eat any of them; she needed to bring them someplace later. I am pleased to tell you that all of the children obeyed their mother and left the cookies alone. The children, however, had their own reasons for obeying their mother's request. Let's check with each child to find out what those reasons were.

First, Amy. Amy could be called "Repay me Amy." Amy, why didn't you have any cookies?

(First child reads.) "Well, I figured that if I did what Mom asked she might

reward me for being so good. She might give me some money or a big bunch of those cookies."

Amy obeyed because she thought she would get something in return for her obedience.

Next, we have Brady. We could call Brady "Fraidy Brady." Brady, why didn't you eat any of those cookies?

(Second child reads.) "It's not because I didn't want any—I *love* cookies. I was afraid that if I had a cookie or two (maybe three), Mom would punish me. She would probably do something awful to me, like make me clean my room."

So Brady was obedient because he was afraid of being punished. He obeyed out of fear.

Finally, we have Sue. We could refer to Sue as "True-blue Sue." Sue, why didn't you eat any of the cookies? Were you afraid you might be punished if you did or rewarded if you didn't? *(Third child reads.)* "No, I love my mom. She told us not to eat the cookies. I love her and want to please her, so I did as she asked."

Sue did what she did out of love.

All three of the children obeyed, but which one of their reasons was the best? *(Responses.)* That's right, Sue. She did it as a response to her love for her mother, not because she was afraid of punishment or wanted to get a reward. This is exactly the same kind of love Jesus wants us to give him. He said, "If you love me, you will keep my commandments." It is my prayer for all of you that you will obey God's commandments out of love for him.   **— D. H.**

The Gospel: John 17:1-11

Focus: Jesus, God's own Son and our Lord, prays for us.

Experience: After talking about how important prayer is, you and the children will focus on the good news that Jesus prays for us.

Jesus Prays for Us

GOD CERTAINLY LOVES TO HAVE US COME TO HIS HOUSE as we have this morning. Here we have an opportunity to hear God's Word, sing songs, and talk to God about many different things. What do we call it when we talk to God? *(Prayer.)* That's right; we call talking to God prayer. God is our very best friend and as our very best friend, he wants us to talk to him often. As we pray in Jesus' name, we can thank God for his many blessings, ask him to forgive us our sins, and pray for others who may have special needs or problems. It's so nice to know that we can talk to our loving God any time, and that he will always hear us.

One very special blessing we have as members of God's family is knowing that there are people who pray for us. When we are sick they pray that we will get better. When we travel they pray that we will have a safe trip. When something good happens in our lives, they thank God for blessing us. Do you have some people who pray for you? *(Responses. Parents, grandparents, others.)* Their prayers for us show that God's love is active in their lives. Do you pray for some people, too, especially when you go to bed at night? *(Responses. Probably family members and friends.)*

In our Gospel for today we heard about Jesus talking to his heavenly Father in prayer. Jesus prayed not only for himself but also for his friends, the disciples. He asked his heavenly Father to watch over them, especially after he returned to heaven. How wonderful it must have been for the disciples to know that Jesus loved them so much that he took time to pray for them.

I have wonderful news for all of you this morning! Jesus, who is very much alive and now with his Father in heaven, is still praying for his disciples, his followers. Who are Jesus' followers today? *(Responses.)* Yes, you and I and all who believe in Jesus as their Lord and Savior are his disciples. Jesus prays for us. He asks God to forgive us our sins and to keep us strong in our faith.

What a wonderful friend we have in Jesus Christ. Not only did he live, die, and rise again for our salvation, but every day he prays to his Father in heaven on our behalf. So pray for others, my young friends, just as Jesus prays for each one of you. — **D. H.**

The Day of Pentecost

The Gospel: John 20:19-23

Focus: As eyewitnesses of the resurrected Christ, Jesus sent his disciples out to tell the world the good news of the gospel as they had seen and heard it.

Experience: The children will hear about an example involving an eyewitness, learn that that the disciples were eyewitnesses who saw and touched the risen Lord, and be encouraged to tell others about Jesus' love.

Preparation: You may use the example of an eyewitness found here or use one of your own. Bring a Bible with you.

Eyewitnesses

TODAY IN OUR GOSPEL LESSON WE HEAR THE EXCITING STORY of Jesus appearing to his disciples after he had risen from the dead on Easter morning. The disciples not only saw Jesus, they touched him too. They knew he was really alive again.

We call someone who has seen something with their own eyes an "eyewitness." We will talk more about what the disciples did after seeing Jesus alive in just a few moments. First, however, let me tell you about a time when I was an eyewitness.

On my way home one afternoon I saw an accident take place right in front of me. A man was driving his car down the street just ahead of me. Then another man, who was coming from a side street, forgot to stop at a stop sign and ran right into the first man's car. Fortunately neither of the drivers was hurt, but both cars were badly dented. I saw the whole thing happen, so I stayed at the scene of the accident to tell the police what I had seen. I was an "eyewitness" because I saw the accident take place. It was my responsibility to describe the accident just as I had seen it happen.

Do you remember how Jesus died? *(Responses. On the cross.)* The disciples were so sad. Can you imagine how excited the disciples must have been when they saw with their own eyes that Jesus was alive? *(Responses. They were very happy.)* Their sadness was changed to great joy when they saw that he was alive.

God, the heavenly Father, had sent Jesus to earth to tell of God's love. Now Jesus told his friends, "As the Father sent me, I am sending you." They were eyewitnesses and he wanted them to go tell others that he was very much alive.

These eyewitnesses not only spent the rest of their lives telling others the good news, but they also wrote it down so that people in years to come would know of God's love in Jesus Christ. We have those eyewitness accounts in this book. What do we call this book? *(The Bible, God's Word.)* That's right.

When someone reads the Bible to us or we read it ourselves, we find out what Jesus did for us. God helps us to have faith in Jesus as our Lord and Savior. Then God gives us the strength and courage to go and tell others about Jesus' love for them.

We are thankful to God for the disciples, those eyewitnesses of the resurrection, for faithfully telling what they had seen and heard. God helps us, too, to be able to tell others about Jesus' love. When you go back to where you are sitting, whisper this to someone close to you, "Jesus loves you." Let's try it now. *(Whisper.)* Jesus loves you. *(Jesus loves you.)* **— D. H.**

The Holy Trinity*

The Gospel: Matthew 28:16-20

Focus: Jesus wants us to teach others what he taught us.

Experience: Some of the children will demonstrate how to tie shoes and tell how they learned that skill. Then they will discuss what Jesus has taught them that they could teach others.

Preparation: Wear or bring shoes with ties in case none of the children are wearing them. Bring paper, a writing surface, and a pencil or pen.

Teaching Others

GOOD MORNING! Let's see what kind of shoes you are wearing. *(Some children may comment.)* Does anyone have shoes with shoelaces? *(If so, ask them to come closer to you. If not, show them the shoes you brought along. Untie those shoes or one of the children's shoes after asking for permission.)*

Who knows how to tie shoes? *(Let volunteers tie the untied shoes.)* How did you learn to tie shoes? *(Responses.)* Were you able to tie your shoes the first time you tried? *(No.)* Most of the time learning to do something new takes time, and most of the time we need someone to show us how. Someone had to teach us to tie our shoes. We don't usually learn how to do it on our own.

How many of you have taught someone else how to tie their shoes? *(Responses.)* What other things have you taught someone how to do? *(How to play games, how to make or fix things, other responses.)*

In the Bible reading today, Jesus told his followers to teach other people to do what he had commanded them. We are Jesus' followers, too. What are some of the things Jesus taught us about how we should treat other people and how to live our lives?

(You may need to ask questions to get them going, such as, "What if someone fell down or got hurt? What did Jesus say about loving each other?" Write down all appropriate responses on your writing surface. If some give inappropriate responses, guide them toward appropriate ones.)

Let's pray. Jesus, thank you for teaching us so many things. *(Read the list.)* Help us to teach other people what you have taught us. Amen. **— C. S.**

---

* First Sunday after Pentecost

The Gospel: Matthew 7:21-29

Focus: We are being wise when we listen to Jesus' words about loving our neighbor as ourselves.

Experience: The children will define *wise* and *foolish*. Then they will hear something Jesus said, listen to you describe some situations, and decide the wise thing to do in each one.

Preparation: Read the situations and change or adapt them to make them more appropriate for your group of children. On one sheet of paper write WISE and draw a smiling face (a circle with two eyes and a smile). On another sheet of paper write FOOLISH and a sad face (a circle with two eyes and a downturned mouth).

Being Wise

TODAY'S GOSPEL LESSON TELLS A STORY ABOUT TWO HOUSES. One was built on sand and the other on a rock. Which house might be in trouble if it rained hard? *(The one on sand.)* You're right! But the one on a rock was safe and wouldn't fall down.

Jesus says that the person who built a house on the rock was wise. *(Hold up the paper with a smiling face and WISE written on it.)* What do you think wise means? *(Smart, practical, sensible.)* Jesus called the person who built a house on the sand foolish. *(Hold up the paper with a sad face and FOOLISH written on it.)* What do you think foolish means? *(Careless, silly, not sensible.)*

Jesus says that wise people are the ones who hear what he says and then do what he says. They are just like the man who built his house upon the rock. In the Bible *(Matthew 22:39b)* Jesus tells us to love our neighbors as ourselves. If we do that, we will be wise. *(Hold up the poster of the smiling face.)*

Let's see if we can think of the wise way to behave in each of these situations. *(Use as many of the following situations as you have time for. After each suggested action, let the children judge the wisdom or foolishness of it. Help them base their decisions on what Jesus said. Encourage possible wise answers and hold up the smiling face.)*

---

* If after Trinity Sunday

— One of the members of your baseball team strikes out during an important game. What could you say to that person? *(Responses.)*

— Your brother or sister knocks over your dad's penny jar. Pennies roll all over the floor. What could you do? *(Responses.)*

— Your mom fixed a big dinner and invited guests. After they leave, she is very tired, but the dirty dishes are piled here and there and things are a mess. What could you do? *(Responses.)*

Let's pray. Jesus, we want to be wise like the man who built his house upon the rock. Help us to do what you say, especially to be loving to other people. Amen. **— C. S.**

The Gospel: Matthew 9:9-13, 18-26

Focus: We are thankful for life and liveliness.

Experience: The children will think about the gift of being alive and being able to do so many enjoyable things.

We Thank God for Our Liveliness

IN THE BIBLE IN MATTHEW'S GOSPEL WE READ ABOUT Jesus healing a girl. How do you think she and her family felt when they realized she was alive and well? *(Happy, thankful, joyful.)*

Life and health are wonderful gifts, aren't they? *(Yes.)* Think of all the things we can do because we are alive and well. *(Ask the children to mention things they can do because they are alive and well. Have them demonstrate what they suggest if appropriate. If there are children with disabilities in your group, try to avoid those actions that they might not be able to do. Try out a few together.)* How can we use our hands and arms? Can we clap? *(You and the children clap.)* Let's wave at some of the people we know in the congregation. *(You and the children wave.)* And we can smile. Let's all smile at them and even blow a few kisses. *(You and the children smile and blow kisses.)* With our voices we can sing and we can talk to our friends and families. Let's tell them, "Jesus loves you." *(All call out, "Jesus loves you!")*

Maybe your moms and dads sometimes complain about your liveliness, but we're so thankful to God that you are all so alive and lively.

Let's pray. God, thank you for our active bodies. Thank you that we are able to *(mention some actions the children talked about or tried)*. We are so happy to be alive and lively. Amen. **— C. S.**

---

* If after Trinity Sunday

Sunday between June 12 and 18 inclusive,*
Proper 6

JUNE 16, 1996   JUNE 13, 1999   JUNE 16, 2002

The Gospel: Matthew 9:35–10:8

Focus: God gives freely to us. We are to give freely to others.

Experience: The.children will look at pictures of things God has given us and consider how much each costs. After deciding that they all cost nothing, they will think of things they could freely give.

Preparation: Bring pictures of at least three of these or similar items: someone showing love, someone giving a hug or a smile, songbirds, a beautiful spring day, rain, sun, a sunrise or sunset, the starry sky, or a rainbow. Invite an older child to read Matthew 10:8b when asked, or be ready to read it yourself. Mark the verse in a Bible.

It's Free

GOOD MORNING. I BROUGHT SOME PICTURES TODAY. *(Show the pictures one at a time. Ask what each one is.)* What do you see in this picture that God has given us? *(Responses.)* How much does *(the item the children mentioned)* cost? *(Bring out the idea that they all are free.)*

Let's listen to what Jesus said. *(Invite the volunteer to read Matthew 10:8b. Thank him or her. Otherwise read it yourself.)* What do you think Jesus is telling us to do? *(Give things to other people without asking them to pay, do kind things for others without expecting to be paid, help for free.)*

It's fine to do jobs and earn money. It's fun to spend and save money, but we shouldn't expect to earn money for every helping or loving thing we do. What are some things that each of you could give freely to someone today? *(Responses might include hugging, smiling, helping with a task, doing a job without being asked, playing with a younger child, and so forth.)*

Let's pray. Thank you, Lord, for the wonderful world and people you've given us. Help us to give our time freely and to share our things with others. Amen. **— C. S.**

---

* If after Trinity Sunday

Sunday between June 19 and 25 inclusive,*
Proper 7

JUNE 23, 1996   JUNE 20, 1999   JUNE 23, 2002

The Gospel: Matthew 10:24-33

Focus: Each of us is precious and valuable to God.

Experience: The children will try to figure out how many hairs are on one child's head. In the process, they will learn how precious they are to God.

Preparation: Bring a calculator, tape measure, something to write on, a pen or pencil, and a Bible. Invite an older child to read Matthew 10:30 when asked, or prepare to read it yourself. Mark that verse in the Bible.

How Many Hairs?

HI! TODAY I NEED A VOLUNTEER. *(Choose someone with short hair who doesn't have it braided or in a ponytail. Invite the volunteer to sit next to you.)* How could we figure out how many hairs are on *(name of volunteer)*'s head? *(Show the children the calculator and measuring tape. Choose one of their ideas and start trying to figure out the problem. After a couple of minutes, continue.)*

(Name of volunteer) has a lot of hair. It might take us a very long time to count all these hairs. Maybe someone already knows how many hairs are on *(name of volunteer)*'s head. *(Ask the volunteer the next question.)* Does anyone in your family know exactly how many hairs are on your head? *(No.)* In the encyclopedia it says that most of us have 100,000 to 150,000 hairs on our head, but that's not an exact number. Let's listen to what Jesus says about our hair. *(Invite the reader to read Matthew 10:30. Thank him or her. Otherwise read it yourself.)*

Jesus tells us that all the hairs on our head have been counted. Who do you think counted them? *(God.)* Why does Jesus tell us that God knows how many hairs are on our heads? *(Jesus wants us to know that God knows all about us; God knows everything.)* Yes, that's right. God knows us so well and loves us so much. Every person is precious and valuable to God, including each one of you!

Let's pray. Dear God, thank you for sending Jesus to tell us how precious and valuable we are. Amen. **— C. S.**

---

* If after Trinity Sunday

Sunday between June 26 and July 2 inclusive, Proper 8

The Gospel: Matthew 10:34-42

Focus: When we welcome others, we are welcoming Jesus.

Experience: The children will talk about how they welcome others at home and in church. Two children will visually illustrate what Jesus says in Matthew 10:40a.

Preparation: Bring a picture of Jesus. Invite an older child to read Matthew 10:40a when asked, or prepare to read it yourself. Mark that verse in a Bible.

Welcome, Jesus!

WELCOME! I'M SO GLAD YOU'RE HERE. What does "welcome" mean? *(Responses. Quite likely they will say, "Hi, hello, glad you're here.")* That's right. A welcome makes the people who just came in feel that we are pleased that they've come. When we welcome someone, we are kind and courteous to them.

What are some ways that you make someone feel welcome in your home? *(Responses. Take their coat, invite them to sit, offer them something to eat or drink, stop our regular activities to spend time with them, and so forth.)* What are some ways that you make people feel welcome in church? *(Responses. Learn their names, show them around, introduce them to others, invite them to visit your home, and so forth.)*

Let's hear what Jesus said about welcoming someone. *(Invite the volunteer to read Matthew 10:40a. Thank him or her. Otherwise read it yourself.)* What did Jesus say? *(When someone welcomes you, they're welcoming Jesus, too.)* Let's see how this works.

(Invite two volunteers to come forward. Give volunteer 2 the picture of Jesus. Ask him or her to hold the picture so that everyone can see Jesus. Ask volunteer 1 to welcome volunteer 2. Once volunteer 2 has been welcomed, continue.)

When *(name of volunteer 1)* welcomed *(name of volunteer 2)*, who else were they welcoming besides *(name of volunteer 2)*? *(Jesus.)*

Let's pray. Lord Jesus, the next time we welcome someone, help us remember that we're welcoming you, too. Amen. **— C. S.**

The Gospel: Matthew 11:25-30

Focus: When we work with Jesus, our burdens become lighter.

Experience: The children will see how much easier it is to pull a heavy object when two are pulling together. They will learn about yokes and consider what it means to take Jesus' yoke.

Preparation: If you can find one, bring a picture of a yoke or a team of animals, such as oxen, yoked together. Fill a box or large container (perhaps a plastic storage crate) with heavy items such as rocks, bricks, or milk jugs filled with water. Attach a rope to the box or container to be used for pulling. Make sure that the box can be pulled without tearing it or the rope becoming detached. Make a place for a second rope to be attached. Bring the second rope, but do not attach it.

Working with Jesus

GOOD MORNING. I HAVE A HEAVY BOX that I'd like a strong volunteer to pull from here to there. *(Indicate where "there" is and choose a volunteer. After the volunteer has pulled or has tried to pull the box, ask the child to describe how it felt.)* I have another rope that I'm going to attach to this box. *(Attach it.)* If two of you pull this box, do you think that it will be easier or harder? *(Most of the children will probably think easier.)* Let's see. *(Choose a second volunteer to take a rope, but whisper to the child to pull in the opposite direction from the first volunteer. Ask the first volunteer:)* Was it was easier or harder to pull the box? *(Harder.)* How could we make it easier? *(The children will probably suggest that the two children need to be pulling together in the same direction. Once they do, have the two volunteers pull the box back to its starting position. Ask this of the first volunteer.)* Now was it easier or harder? *(Easier.)* That's right. Working together makes a job easier.

(Show the picture of the yoke if you found one.) What is this and what it is used for? *(If you don't have a picture, describe a yoke to them.)* A yoke fastens two animals together, perhaps oxen, so that they work as a team. Without a yoke, the animals might try to go in opposite directions and wouldn't get any work done. With the yoke on, the animals work together and the job becomes easier.

Jesus talked about a yoke. He said his yoke is easy and his burden is light.

What do you think Jesus meant? *(They may not be sure, so continue explaining.)* If we imagine ourselves yoked to Jesus so that he is our partner, our life won't be as difficult as it might be if we tried to do everything by ourselves. Jesus is always with us. Jesus helps us. We can pray to him any time.

Let's pray. Jesus, thank you for wanting us to be by your side. Thank you for helping us. Amen. **— C. S.**

Sunday between July 10 and 16 inclusive, Proper 10

JULY 14, 1996   JULY 11, 1999   JULY 14, 2002

The Gospel: Matthew 13:1-9

Focus: Through the parable of the soil we learn that God wants us to listen so that we know what God wants us to do.

Experience: By the use of visual images, the children will think about how well they listen to God's Word.

Preparation: Bring two ears of corn and an indoor television antenna (rabbit ears) or pictures or drawings of them.

Listen Up!

DO YOU KNOW WHAT THESE TWO THINGS HAVE IN COMMON? *(Show the ears of corn and the "rabbit ears" or pictures of them.)* They both have the word "ear" in their names. These are ears of corn, and these are called rabbit ears. Their names are about all that they have in common.

These ears, which are ears of corn, can't hear a thing. These rabbit ears hear very well. Old television sets always had them. Have any of you ever seen them? *(Responses.)* They would pick up sounds and pictures from the air and change them so people could watch and listen to their TVs. They are called rabbit ears because, like a real rabbit's ears, they stick up into the air and hear very well. Hearing all sorts of sounds helps the rabbit to protect itself.

In our Bible story today, Jesus says that some people listen to God's Word as though they had ears of corn in their head instead of real ears. *(Put the ears of corn up to the sides of your head.)* They don't hear anything. Other people listen very closely when they hear somebody tell them about God. It is as if they have rabbit ears in their heads. *(Put rabbit ears on top of your head.)* They want to hear everything so they can try to do what God wants. And yes, there are some people who have an ear of corn in one ear *(hold an ear of corn on one side of your head)* and a rabbit ear on the other *(hold rabbit ears on other side of your head)*. They only half listen, and if you ask them what was just said, they get all mixed up trying to tell you what they heard.

Jesus says that God needs people who listen with ears as well as rabbit ears to what God wants them to do. So when you get up in the morning or when you go to bed at night, pray a prayer of thanks to God. Then you could add some other words to God. Say what I say: "Speak, God." *(Speak, God.)* "I am listening." *(I am listening.)* God speaks to you through the Bible and in

Sunday school and church, through other people telling you about God, and in many ways. Once again, let's say, "Speak, God, I am listening." *(Speak, God, I am listening.)* **—W.Y.**

The Gospel: Matthew 13:24-30

Focus: As it is difficult to separate wheat and weeds because they look alike, so it is difficult to distinguish a good person from a bad person. Only God can judge, and that judgment is reserved for the end of history.

Experience: The children will realize that it is wrong to judge others because they themselves would not like to be judged. They will learn that only God can judge.

Preparation: You could bring pictures or examples of garden plants and weeds.

Avoiding Judgment

WHEN ARE OTHER PEOPLE HARD TO LIVE WITH? Can you tell me about the times when other people bug you? *(When they don't share. When they say things I don't like. When they lie. Other responses.)* When people do things that bug you, do you have very good thoughts about them? *(No.)*

Now let me ask you another question. When are the times that you are hard to live with? When do other people say you bug them? *(When I leave my toys all over. When I stay in the bathroom too long. When I yell. Other responses.)* When you bug other people, do you think that they have good thoughts or bad thoughts about you? *(Bad thoughts.)* I agree, they probably have bad thoughts, since we have bad thoughts about them when they bug us.

We all do things that bug other people, and then we are hard to live with. That does not mean that just because people are hard to live with they are bad people. God doesn't think of them that way, and God doesn't think of us that way. God loves us all and wants to help us to love ourselves when we are hard to live with. God wants to help others to feel loved, too.

We don't want anybody to think of us as a bad person when we are hard to live with, and it would be wrong for us to think of somebody who bugged us as a bad person. Jesus says that we must learn to live with one another and tolerate one another's mistakes. God will help us to be able to do good things so that we don't bug others so much.

Separating people into good people and bad people is like trying to figure out which plants are weeds and which ones are vegetables or flowers in the garden in the springtime. Do any of your families plant gardens or flower beds in spring? Is it sometimes hard to tell which are plants we want and which are weeds? *(Responses. Show examples or pictures if you brought some.)* It is hard to judge, especially about people. It is best to let God be the judge. And remember that before God judges us, he is there to help us, forgive us, and love us. **—W.Y.**

The Gospel: Matthew 13:44-52

Focus: In the parable of the pearl of great price, Jesus makes us consider what we are willing to give up in order to have something that is really valuable.

Experience: Using hand motions, the children will experience the excitement of throwing away what is of little value to them and the fun of claiming something of great value.

Preparation: Bring a strand of pearls or other pearl jewelry.

Throwing Things Away

HAVE YOU EVER LOST SOMETHING you loved so much that you spent the whole day looking for it? *(Responses.)* Have you ever seen your parents looking for something that they could not find? Did they practically tear the house down while looking for it? *(Responses.)*

Jesus once told a story, which we call a parable, about a trader who traded in fine pearls like these pearls here. *(Show necklace or jewelry.)* Jesus said that this trader of fine pearls was always looking for the perfect pearl, just as someone who collects baseball cards might look for a rookie Frank Thomas card or Mickey Mantle card *(substitute another example if you wish).* If the trader found the almost perfect pearl, Jesus said that the trader would sell everything in the store to get the money to buy that almost-perfect pearl.

So it is that when we find God's love in our hearts, we are happy. But then we want to throw quite a few things out of our hearts in order to make more room for the love of God. We start by throwing out things that really don't belong there. We will be sure to throw out the bad moods we sometimes have when we are really grumpy *(use hand motions to pretend to throw things out and invite children to do the same)* and any ugly thoughts that hide inside us *(hand motions).* Do any of you ever have those grumpy times? *(Responses.)* We will throw out selfishness, when we grab first and want the biggest piece of cake *(hand motions),* and laziness and hate, because we would want to make sure that there is room in our hearts for God's love.

We might even throw out whatever is inside us that makes us whine *(hand motions)* and tease and complain. We will get rid of everything we can to make room for lots of love. We want love in our hearts, because love will always make room for Jesus. **—W.Y.**

The Gospel: Matthew 14:13-21

Focus: Through one young person's offering of five loaves of bread and two fish, Jesus was able to feed a multitude.

Experience: Through the use of a calculator, the children will multiply the number of meals they have eaten in a lifetime and realize that the gifts of God are too many to count. They will also realize that the gifts we give to God multiply when God puts them to use.

Preparation: Bring a calculator.

Multiplying the Gifts of God

TODAY WE READ IN THE GOSPEL LESSON from the Scriptures that a young boy offered his lunch of five loaves and two fish to Jesus so that he could feed a crowd that had come to hear him. After Jesus blessed the food by thanking God for it, he asked the disciples to distribute the food. More than five thousand people were fed, and there were still twelve baskets of food left over after the meal. What the young person gave to Jesus was multiplied many times, wasn't it? *(Yes.)*

Have you ever thought about how many meals you have eaten in your lifetime? How many times do you think you have eaten, not including snacks? *(Responses.)*

I have my calculator here, and by using it, I can tell you how many meals you have eaten in your lifetime. Most people around here eat three meals a day, and if I multiply by three times the 365 days in a year, my calculator tells me how many that is. Can one of you read this number for me? *(1,095.)* Most people here eat about 1,095 meals every year. Wow!

If you are five years old, I can multiply 1,095 times five and get what? *(5,475.)* You five-year-olds have eaten 5,475 meals in your life, not including the extra times you ate when you were a baby or the snack times you have now.

I can do this for each age: Three-year-olds have eaten 3,285 times, four-year-olds have eaten 4,380 times, six-year-olds 6,570 times, seven-year-olds 7,665 times, and eight-year-olds more than 8,520 meals. *(Add other ages and amounts as needed.)*

Imagine how many times your parents have eaten! If your mother or father is thirty-five or so, she or he has eaten more than 38,000 meals already.

Now think of this. The food for every one of these meals has come from God. We thank God for giving us this food when we say grace, when we pray before we eat. God is very generous and really likes to share. More than one thousand times a year God gives us a meal. We are really thankful, so that is why we pray prayers of thanks when we sit down to eat.

And think of this. One young person shared his lunch of five loaves and two fish with Jesus, and Jesus offered the food to God. When God gave the food back, it had multiplied enough times to feed more than five thousand people. God is very generous. Remember that when we share with God, what we share gets multiplied! **— W.Y.**

The Gospel: Matthew 14:22-33

Focus: In the story of Jesus calling Peter to walk to him on the sea, we learn that keeping our focus on Jesus can help us pass over troubled waters.

Experience: By hearing the story of Ruby Bridges* walking between U.S. marshals into a previously all-white school, the children may begin to appreciate the value of lessons learned at church and realize the importance of Jesus in their lives.

Preparation: If you have access to a reproduction of Norman Rockwell's *The Problem We All Live With*, it will provide a visual image to reinforce the story of Ruby Bridges.

Jesus Is Our Lifeline

THERE WAS A TIME IN OUR COUNTRY, GIRLS AND BOYS, when white children and black children did not attend school together as they do today. You probably know that. Then the United States government decided that children would get a better education if all races of children could attend school together. This change was difficult for many people to accept, and some kept their children home from school out of fear or prejudice.

In 1960 there was one six-year-old black girl named Ruby who showed a lot of courage when she went to a school that used to be only for white children. She had to walk between federal police officers to be safe because many angry white people stood along the sidewalk where she walked. They yelled at Ruby and insulted her and even spit at her.

For many months she was the only person who attended her class because all the other students stayed home. You can imagine how scared she was to get up each morning to go to school. But Ruby didn't give up. She walked straight to school every day without saying a word to anyone.

How do you think she took her mind off the bad things people were saying about her so she could walk straight to school? *(Responses.)* Dr. Coles, a counselor who talked to Ruby Bridges many times, says that she prayed a lot.

---

* This story is told by Robert Coles in *The Moral Life of Children* (Boston: Atlantic Monthly Press, 1986) 22–27.

He says that she prayed each night and each morning and sometimes on the way to school. She prayed that God would help the people that didn't like her. In church Ruby learned to do what Jesus said, and when she went to school, she remembered Jesus. She knew Jesus was with her.

I wonder if she knew the story that we read today from the Bible about Peter trying to walk on the water to Jesus during a storm. Jesus promised to reach out for Peter as he walked on the water with the rain coming down and the wind blowing. But every time a gust of wind came by, Peter turned to the wind instead of looking at Jesus, and he would sink down into the water. Finally Jesus had to come toward him and catch him to keep him from drowning.

Ruby Bridges never forgot the stories of the Bible. She trusted Jesus, too. We, too, can trust Jesus to help us and be with us when we face trouble. He will help us as he helped Peter and as he helped Ruby Bridges. **—W.Y.**

Sunday between August 14 and 20 inclusive, Proper 15

AUG. 18, 1996   AUG. 15, 1999   AUG. 18, 2002

The Gospel: Matthew 15:21-28

Focus: Jesus will help you.

Experience: You and the children will talk about what it means to ask for help.

Jesus, Help Me

TODAY'S BIBLE STORY IS ABOUT A WOMAN who asked Jesus to help her. What does it mean to ask for help? *(Responses.)* What are some things you need help with? *(Responses. You can offer hints about getting things down from high places, tying shoes, carrying heavy things, reading, and so forth.)* What are some things you can help others with? *(Responses. If needed, prompt with ideas such as caring for a brother or sister, picking up toys, setting the table, and so forth.)*

It's great to be able to ask for help sometimes. But sometimes it's hard to ask for help, isn't it? *(Yes.)* And sometimes we have to do things that are so hard that it seems no one could help us.

In today's Bible story, there was a woman whose daughter was very sick. She was very worried. She didn't know how to help her daughter. But she had heard about Jesus and she knew he was near. So she came to Jesus and said, "Have mercy on me, Lord, Son of David; my daughter is tormented by a demon." Jesus didn't recognize the woman. She wasn't one of his followers. But she was desperate. She knelt down and asked him over and over, "Lord, help me."

It wasn't easy for her to ask for help, but she believed that Jesus cared for her and her daughter, even though they were not his friends or followers.

And she was right. Jesus did care for her. Jesus answered her, "Woman, great is your faith! Let it be done for you as you wish." And do you know what? At that very moment, her daughter became well.

Do you ever think of asking Jesus to help you? *(Responses. If no one says yes, ask them to consider situations where they might ask for help: when they are sick, lonely, or frightened.)* Jesus cares for you, and you can always ask him for help. And afterwards, when things are better, remember to thank him.

Let's pray. Thank you, Jesus, for caring for us. We are happy that you are always there to help us. Thank you. Amen. — **L. R.**

The Gospel: Matthew 16:13-20

Focus: In Jesus' day, people learned who he was by watching what he did. We can also know who Jesus is by hearing what the Bible says about what he did.

Experience: The children will look at several different pictures and guess, from the pictures, what the person does for a living.

Preparation: From magazines and newspapers, cut pictures of people doing various things (*pilot, teacher, carpenter, pastor, bus driver*). The children should easily be able to identify the person's job from the picture.

Who Is Jesus?

TODAY I WANT TO SHOW YOU SOME PICTURES. Each picture has some clues about who the person is and what he or she does. Look carefully and see if you can guess what each person's job is. (*Hold them up one at a time. Invite the children to tell what they see and encourage them to make some observations about the person.*)

That's interesting. Even though you have never met any of these people, you knew what kind of job each person had. How did you know that? (*By looking at what they were doing.*) That's right, by looking at what they were doing.

You know, the same thing was true of Jesus. One day, Jesus asked his disciples who people thought he was. The disciples gave him lots of different answers. Some people thought Jesus was like one of the prophets from the old days in Israel. Others thought he might be a new version of John the Baptist.

Jesus also asked his disciples, "But who do you say that I am?" Peter, one of the disciples, gave a new and more important answer: "You are the Messiah, the Son of the living God."

Remember how you guessed the people's jobs by looking at pictures? The people around Jesus had seen what he did and they made some guesses—he was a prophet who spoke God's Word, or a great teacher, or a healer, and things like that. But Peter knew even more; he said Jesus was really God's own Son.

When we read the Bible and hear Bible stories, we also can see that Jesus was not just a teacher or prophet. He healed people, loved people, and finally died on the cross for us. Jesus is God's own Son, our Savior.

Who is Jesus? Let's say those words together. Jesus is God's own Son, our Savior. *(Jesus is God's own Son, our Savior.)*

Let's pray. Thank you, God, for sending your Son, Jesus. Help us to learn more and more about him, so that we can tell other people about him too. Amen. **— L. R.**

Sunday between August 28 and September 3 inclusive, Proper 17

SEPT. 1, 1996   AUG. 29, 1999   SEPT. 1, 2002

The Gospel: Matthew 16:21-26

Focus: Being a Christian means following Jesus and doing as Jesus would do.

Experience: You and the children will play "Simon Says."

Preparation: Practice your statements ahead of time.

Followers of Jesus

LET'S PLAY A GAME TOGETHER. Have you ever played "Simon Says"? *(Responses.)* I will tell you to do something. If I say, "Simon says," then you should do it right away. But if I don't say, "Simon says," then don't do it. Ready?

Simon says touch your nose. *(Allow time for them to do so.)* Good. Simon says clap your hands. *(Allow time for them to do so.)* All right. Simon says, say "praise God." *(Allow time for them to do so.)* Now raise your hand. *(Tailor your comments, depending on whether anyone followed your directions. Remind them that you did not say, "Simon says.")*

Playing "Simon Says" is just a game. But when you do what Simon says, it shows that you are listening.

Jesus told people that if they wanted to become his followers, they had to deny themselves and take up their cross and follow him. Jesus was telling his disciples that to follow him, they had to listen to him and be willing to do what he did.

What are some of the things Jesus did for people? *(Responses. He healed people, taught them, prayed for them, loved them. If necessary, prompt them by asking questions such as, "How did he treat people? Did he love them?" Yes. "Care for them?" Yes. "Did he forgive them?" Yes.)* That's right.

If Jesus were playing "Simon Says" with you, he might say, "Jesus says love one another. Jesus says care for one another. Jesus says forgive one another." When we do as Jesus says, we show we are his followers.

Let's pray. Thank you, Jesus, for coming to show us how to live. Help us to follow you each day. Amen. **— L. R.**

Sunday between September 4 and 10 inclusive, Proper 18

SEPT. 8, 1996   SEPT. 5, 1999   SEPT. 8, 2002

The Gospel: Matthew 18:15-20

Focus: Jesus wants us to live in harmony together and to love one another always.

Experience: You and the children will talk about what to do when you disagree with someone.

Preparation: Use the story given here, or think of a simple instance in which someone did something you disagreed with and how you resolved your differences. It could be a story from your childhood or involve children in some way.

Love One Another

TO BEGIN TODAY, I WANT TO TELL YOU A STORY. *(Tell your own brief story about an instance of disagreement and resolution. If you cannot think of one, use the following.)* When I was little, I had a friend named Debbie. I really liked her, but one day when we played together we had an argument and I ran home crying. My mom told me to go back and talk it over with Debbie. I did, but Debbie wouldn't listen to me. Finally mom went with me. We talked about how we felt, and after a while we agreed to play together again. Because we talked it over, we could stay friends.

Has anything like that ever happened to you? Has anyone ever done something to you that you thought was wrong? *(Responses.)* When someone does something you disagree with, should you hit the person? Should you just scream at them? Should you slam the door or stomp away mad? Should you refuse to talk to them again? *(No.)* What can you do when you disagree with someone? *(Responses. Prompt them as needed. Encourage them to think of ways to talk and work out their differences.)*

In today's Bible reading, Jesus taught his disciples what people should do when they disagree. He says that when someone does something you disagree with, you need to talk to the person and let them know how you feel. If your friend did something that you disagreed with and your friend refused to listen to you, what could you do? *(Responses.)* Sometimes it helps if you explain your problem to someone else and ask that person to go with you to talk to your friend.

Jesus tells us that when we disagree with someone, we need to talk it over and try to work things out. And if talking doesn't work, what can we do? *(Love, forgive, get someone to go with us to help, and pray for those we disagree with.)*

Let's pray. Thank you, Jesus, for always loving us. Help us always to love others too. Amen. **— L. R.**

Sunday between September 11 and 17 inclusive, Proper 19

SEPT. 15, 1996   SEPT. 12, 1999   SEPT. 15, 2002

The Gospel: Matthew 18:21-35

Focus: Jesus' command to forgive has no limits.

Experience: By seeing what seventy times seven looks like, the children will begin to see that there is no limit to the forgiveness they should extend to others.

Preparation: On a piece of posterboard, draw the following diagram. On one side of the posterboard, make seven bold, straight lines. On the other side make seventy groups of seven lines—seven groups across and ten down, a total of 490 lines.

Seventy Times Seven

HAVE YOU EVER HAD SOMETHING HAPPEN when someone broke one of your toys or ruined something of yours? *(Responses.)* Let's pretend that I borrowed your favorite video game and by accident, I ruined it. Could you forgive me? *(The children will probably say yes. If they don't, you could respond by saying, "It might be hard to forgive me for breaking your game, but if it was an accident and I didn't mean to do it and I would replace the game, would you forgive me then?" Chat with the children until they can agree that they would forgive you.)*

Now, let's imagine that I asked to borrow another game from you and you agreed. But, can you believe it, it happened again. By accident, I ruined that game, too. Do you think you could forgive me? *(Responses. Continue in this manner for a few more times. It may be increasingly difficult for the children to say they forgive you, and that is fine.)*

It is always a little hard to forgive someone, but what's even harder is to *keep on* forgiving someone, right?

In Jesus' day, there was a custom. When someone did something wrong to you, you were to forgive them, and not just once. You were to forgive them up to seven times, but after that you didn't need to forgive them anymore. Seven times. That's a lot, isn't it? If I borrowed your video games seven times and broke them seven times and said I was sorry seven times and you forgave me seven times, that would be a lot of forgiveness, wouldn't it? *(Yes.)* If we were keeping track on a piece of paper, this is what seven looks like. *(Show the posterboard and count the seven strikes.)*

But do you know what? Jesus thought that even seven times was not enough. In today's Bible story, Jesus told his disciples they should not forgive just seven times. He said they should be willing to forgive seventy times seven. Wow. Do any of you know how much seventy times seven is? *(490.)* That's right. And that's a lot. Look at these. *(Show the posterboard with the seventy-times-seven diagram.)* But do you know, when Jesus said seventy times seven, it was his way of saying that we should always be willing to forgive. Always. No matter how many times.

And do you know what? That is how God treats us. God doesn't keep score of the bad things we do. God doesn't write down each time he forgives us. God loves us completely and forgives us always.

And that's the good news for today. Let's pray. Thank you, God, for always loving us, and always forgiving us. Help us to be forgiving, too. Amen. **— L. R.**

Sunday between September 18 and 24 inclusive, Proper 20

SEPT. 22, 1996   SEPT. 19, 1999   SEPT. 22, 2002

The Gospel: Matthew 20:1-16

Focus: God loves all people equally.

Experience: You and the children will talk about fairness and unfairness.

Preparation: Make a sign that says, "Needed: Workers. $10.00 a day."

God Wants You

GOOD MORNING! TODAY, I WANT YOU TO PRETEND that you are all looking for a job, and I am looking for workers. See, I have a sign here. Can you read what it says? *(Responses. Help as needed.)* So that means I want people to come and help me paint the walls of the rooms in my apartment and I will give them $10.00 for each day they work for me. That's a pretty good deal, isn't it? *(Responses.)*

(As you speak, divide the group into three to five smaller groups or individuals, depending on the number of children.) Now, let's pretend that I hired you to paint my apartment *(indicate about one-fourth of the group)* and that I agreed to pay you ten dollars for working the whole day. OK. The apartment is over here. *(Indicate an area.)* Now you pretend you are painting. *(Encourage them to pantomime painting so that those who start first may actually feel tired when they are done.)*

A little later in the day, I decided I needed more workers, so I hired you to paint my apartment, too *(indicate another one-fourth of the group)*, and I agreed to pay you ten dollars for working, even though it won't be a whole day. OK. You paint this room. *(Indicate an area.)* Now you pretend you are painting.

(Continue in this manner until you have "hired" all the children, perhaps four groups in all. With the last two groups, emphasize that even though it is later in the day, you will pay them the same amount that you paid the workers who have been there all day long. Check in with the earlier groups and ask whether they are getting tired yet, and encourage them to keep on going. Try to emphasize the apparent unfairness and allow the children to express their discomfort or disagreement with your plan.)

Now let's pretend this is the end of the day. No matter how long you have been painting, I pay you all the same. *(Pretend to hand out money.)* Some of you have worked six or eight hours. Some of you only worked one or two hours. That doesn't seem quite fair, does it? *(Responses. Help them see that some people had to work harder for their payment.)* That isn't really fair, but that is what I decided to do. *(Have the children sit down.)*

Do you know what? This is how God treats us. God wants us to believe in him, love him, and follow him. But you know, not all people learn about God at the same time. Some people learn about God when they are little children. They hear stories from the Bible and they learn that God loves them. And they learn that God wants to be with them, not just here on earth but in heaven forever.

Just think. How old are you now? *(Responses.)* Let's pretend that you will live for one hundred more years. That means you could believe in God for *(add someone's age to one hundred)* years! That's a long, long time. And when your life on earth is done, God wants to welcome you home to heaven.

But you know, God loves all people and wants all people to be with him. That means that some other people might live most of their lives without knowing God or hearing about Jesus. They might never have the chance to learn that God sent Jesus to be their Savior. They might live one hundred years and never hear the story, but then one day, someone might read the Bible to them, or tell them the story of God's love, and they might say, "I believe it, and I know God loves me." When their life on earth is over, God wants to welcome them home to heaven, too.

That might not seem quite fair. Some people might think they deserve more because they spent more time learning about God. But the gift of God's love is for all people. And God wants all people to be with him. We can be thankful that our God is a God of love and forgiveness who wants us to be with him.

Let's pray. Heavenly Father, thank you for loving us and wanting us to be with you always. Help us to tell others about you so that they can know and love you, too. Amen. **— L. R.**

Sunday between September 25 and October 1 inclusive, Proper 21

SEPT. 29, 1996   SEPT. 26, 1999   SEPT. 29, 2002

The Gospel: Matthew 21:28-32

Focus: Our words are important, but our actions speak louder than our words.

Experience: The children will act out the parable of the two sons.

Preparation: Review the story and think about how you could help the children to act it out. Think about specific Christian service opportunities available in your congregation, such as a food shelf, mission projects, and other caregiving ministries.

Show Me

HOW MANY OF YOU KNOW WHAT CHORES ARE? *(Responses.)* Do you have any chores to do? *(Responses.)* That's great. It's a good feeling to be able to help out, isn't it? *(Yes.)*

I'm wondering, when someone asks you to do a chore, do you always say yes? *(Accept their responses, but encourage them to say no, honestly.)* How about if you would rather be doing something else? How about when you've just finished doing other chores? How about when your brother or sister was supposed to do this chore? Sometimes we feel like saying no, right? *(Yes.)*

I need your help. *(Divide the group into two groups. Be sure that all are seated.)* This will be the "yes" group and this will be the "no" group. I'm going to ask each group some questions, and I want you always to answer yes, and you always to answer no, but nobody should move. Ready?

In today's Bible story, Jesus told a story about a man who had two sons. One of the sons liked to please the father. No matter what the father asked, he always said yes, but he didn't do what he promised.

Let me show you how this worked. Let's pretend. *(Talk to the "yes" group.)* I need some extra seats for people during worship. Would you be willing to stand up through the rest of the service so they could sit in your place? *(Encourage them to say yes, but remind them not to move.)* Will you do it right away? *(Yes.)* Isn't that nice? *(Yes.)* But there was one problem. Even though the son always said yes, he did not always do what he said he would. Even though he said yes, his actions said no, just like our "yes" group.

The other son was grumpier. It seemed that no matter what the father asked, the son would usually say no. *(Talk to the "no" group.)* I need some extra seats for people during worship. Would you be willing to stand up through the rest of the service so they could sit in your place? *(Encourage them to say no.)* Please? *(No.)* Are you sure? *(No.)* But you know, something funny happened. Even though the son would say no, he would usually feel bad about his grumpy attitude, and he would end up doing what his father asked after all. *(Signal this group to stand up.)* See how it works? You can sit down again because we are only pretending.

One day, the father went to the first son and asked *(address the "no" group)*, "Will you go and work in the vineyard today?" And the grumpy son said *(signal the "no" group to say no)*. But later he changed his mind and went to work.

Later the father went to the other son and asked *(address the "yes" group)*, "Will you go and work in the vineyard today?" And the other son said *(signal them to say yes)*. But even though the son said he would go to the vineyard, he did not go.

Now which of these two children really did what the father asked? The one who said yes and didn't go, or the one who said no but did go? *(The one who said no but who did go.)* That's right.

When someone asks you to do something, it's important to say yes, but it is also important to do as you promise. That is true when people ask us to do something, and it is true when God asks us to do something. It is important that when we say we love God, our actions show love, too.

What are some ways we can show others we love God? *(Responses. Think about specific opportunities available in your congregation, such as a food shelf, mission projects, and other caregiving ministries, and prompt as necessary. Be as concrete as possible.)*

That's right. In all of these things, we are saying with our words that we love God and showing it with our actions.

Let's pray. Thank you, God, for the chance to be together today. Help us to learn about you more and more so that we can hear your word and show our love for you. Amen. **— L. R.**

The Gospel: Matthew 21:33-46

Focus: Jesus supports us and holds us together.

Experience: The children will see how building blocks work together and are supported by one another.

Preparation: Bring some wooden building blocks.

Building Blocks

LOOK WHAT I BROUGHT TODAY. *(Pour out the blocks in a central area.)* Building blocks. How many of you have ever made something with blocks? *(Responses.)* Each one of these blocks is important, but if we use them all together we can make something much bigger. Let's try to make something together. *(Allow about one minute for them to work together as much as possible, but try to include all the children, directing the construction as needed. The building should be tall enough so that later when you remove one of the lower blocks, the building will tumble down.)*

Looking at this building of blocks reminds me about our church. Look out there. Is there one person? *(No.)* That's right. There are many people, many people working together and caring for one another. That is what helps to make a church. If there was only one person, would we have a church? *(No. Not really.)*

Who else is part of our church? I'm thinking of someone you cannot see. *(Jesus.)* That's right. Jesus is always with us. In fact, if Jesus were not with us, we would not have a church. Jesus calls us to worship, and the Bible teaches us about him. Who are some of the people who teach us about Jesus? *(Friends, teachers, parents, pastor, and so on.)* That's right. All of us, working together, are the church.

Look at our building blocks. Together they make a building, but what would happen if I removed this block? *(Point to a block on the bottom row that would cause the structure to tumble down. Wait for their responses.)* That's right. That block could be called a cornerstone. It helps to hold up all of the others. Let's move it and see what happens. *(Remove the block and let the blocks tumble.)*

A cornerstone helps to hold up a building. And Jesus is like that cornerstone. In the Bible story today we read, "The stone that the builders rejected has become the cornerstone; this was the Lord's doing, and it is amazing in our eyes." Jesus is the cornerstone that holds our church together. When our church is gathered around Jesus, then we have a strong and healthy church. But without Jesus, we can't do much of anything.

Let's pray. Thank you, Jesus, for being with us in our church. Help us all to work together and love one another. Amen. — **L. R.**

The Gospel: Matthew 22:1-10

Focus: God invites everyone to be members of his holy family. He uses his Word to extend that invitation and asks us to help him.

Experience: The children will look at a contemporary wedding invitation and talk about its purpose. Then they will learn that the Bible is God's invitation to all to become members of his holy family. Our role, as members of his family, is faithfully to extend his invitation to others.

Preparation: Bring a wedding invitation and a Bible.

Delivering God's Invitation

HOW MANY OF YOU HAVE EVER GONE with your family to a wedding? *(Responses).* How did you know when and where the wedding would take place? *(As the children respond, give hints, if necessary, about receiving a wedding invitation.)* You are absolutely right! Your parents received a wedding invitation like this one. *(Show them the invitation you brought with you.)* The invitation told them not only who was getting married but also when and where the wedding would take place.

A wedding is a very joyful occasion for the man and woman who are getting married. They want their friends and family there to celebrate with them as they proclaim their love for one another. Unfortunately, not everyone who is invited will attend the wedding, but they receive an invitation just the same.

In our Gospel lesson for today, Jesus told his disciples a story to give them an idea of what heaven would be like. He told them that heaven would be like a wonderful wedding celebration. God the Father will give the banquet for his Son Jesus, who is the groom. If Jesus is the groom, who do you think the bride is? *(Responses. The children may not know.)* The bride is the church, and the church is people, it is us, it is everyone who believes in Jesus as their Lord and Savior. Because of God's gracious love for us in sending his Son, Jesus, to live, die, and rise again for our salvation, we are all invited to this wonderful banquet. Won't heaven be great!

Where did all of you learn of God's great love for you? *(Responses.)* That's right—at home, in Sunday school, and here in church. The pastor, your Sunday school teachers, and your parents shared God's Word with you. We find God's Word in this book that we call the Bible. *(Hold up a Bible.)* God's invitation for us to become members of his family is found in the Bible. Every time the Word of God is shared, God is extending his invitation to those who hear it to come and be members of his holy family.

God wants us to tell others who may not know about his great love for them. Who do you suppose he wants to help him in sharing the good news? *(Responses.)* Yes, he wants us to share his invitation with those who do not know him. We do this every time we tell someone about Jesus. When you go back to your seats, why not tell someone there, "God loves you!" Let's say it together. *(God loves you!)* So take God's Word, his invitation to become members of his holy family, and share its good news with others. **— D. H.**

Sunday between October 16 and 22 inclusive, Proper 24

OCT. 20, 1996   OCT. 17, 1999   OCT. 20, 2002

The Gospel: Matthew 22:15-21

Focus: We are citizens of two places, our own country and also God's kingdom, but belonging to God's kingdom is more important.

Experience: You and the children will talk about Jesus' words about paying taxes to Caesar and about being citizens of two places.

Preparation: Bring some quarters and a Bible.

Citizens of Two Places

TODAY THE GOSPEL STORY IS ABOUT some people who asked Jesus whether or not they should pay taxes to Caesar, their ruler. Jesus told them to look at the coin they had and see whose face was shown on it. There was a picture, an engraving, of Caesar's face. Jesus said to go ahead and give to Caesar what was Caesar's; his face was on the coin. So he was saying they *should* pay taxes to their government. But then he added, "Give to God the things that are God's."

Look at these quarters I brought along. *(Pass them around.)* Is there a face on them? *(Yes.)* That's Thomas Jefferson, president of the United States a long time ago. *(Alter as needed for Canada or other countries.)* When I buy something, maybe a present for someone's birthday *(name a toy or something the children like)*, I have to pay sales tax. So these quarters might go to the government for taxes! We don't like to pay taxes, but that's what we need to do as citizens of our country.

(Collect the quarters again and tell the children that this time the coins will go in the offering plate instead of going to the government as taxes.) What is the name of the country we live in? *(The United States of America, Canada, and so forth.)* That's right. We should be good citizens of our country, obeying its laws, voting when we are old enough, and doing other things that help our country. But we are also citizens of God's kingdom, and Jesus says that is even more important.

So you are a citizen of two places. We mentioned what we do as citizens of our country, but now we need to think about what it means to be citizens of God's kingdom. That may be difficult, because God's kingdom is much *bigger*. It even includes heaven.

Do we have a book, or teachers, or anything that can help us know what it means to be citizens of God's kingdom? Do you think this book can help us? What do we call it? *(The Bible.)* The Bible helps us, and so does this church, and our pastor and teachers and parents. The main thing they all tell us is how much God loves us, so much that he sent Jesus to be our Savior. And the main thing they tell us to do is to be loving, too.

So we are citizens of two places, our country and God's kingdom, and guess which one is more important. I'll give you a hint; it's the one that is bigger than the other. *(God's kingdom.)* That's right. We belong first and foremost to God, and even though God's kingdom is very big, God knows each one of you and loves each one of you. That is wonderful news, isn't it?
— D. H.

The Gospel: Matthew 22:34-40

Focus: True Christian love begins as we love the Lord our God with all our heart and with all our soul and with all our mind.

Experience: The children will learn, through a number of examples, that in order to accomplish many activities we must start with the important first step. The most important place for Christians to begin is by loving God with all that is in us.

Preparation: You may wish to bring the following: a ladder, a cake mix, and a telephone.

Where Love Begins

JESUS SPOKE OFTEN OF THE IMPORTANCE OF LOVE in the lives of his followers. Since love is so important to him, it should also be important to us. Where does love begin for us, as God's people? We are going to answer that question in a few moments, but first we are going to look at some other activities and ask you where or how we should begin them.

I have here a ladder. *(If you didn't bring one, describe one.)* If I want to use my ladder to help me trim some branches from the tree in front of my house, I need to do some things. What if I jump to the middle step on my ladder or maybe jump all the way to the very top? Would that be a good idea? *(Responses.)* No, of course not. Where would I begin in climbing the ladder? *(Responses.)*

You are absolutely right! After setting my ladder up, I would begin climbing it by stepping on the first step and then going step by step as high as I wish to go.

Here is a telephone. *(Show telephone.)* My friend would like for me to call him and talk about a trip we have planned. How would I go about doing that? Would I simply pick up the telephone and begin talking to my friend? *(Responses.)* Obviously that won't work. What do I have to do first? How do I begin? *(Responses.)* Certainly! I have to dial my friend's number and wait for him to answer before I can speak with him on the telephone.

I sure do like cake! How many of you like cake, too? *(Responses.)* You will be pleased to know that I have a cake mix right here. *(Show them the cake mix.)* I'll just open the box, dump what's inside into a pan, and we'll eat this cake. Does that sound like a good idea? *(Responses.)* So you don't think that is a very good idea? What should I do first? How do I begin? *(Responses.)* Once again, you are right. After I open the box, I have to mix all the ingredients together, put the batter in a pan, and bake it in an oven if I want to have a cake.

Let's get back to the question that I asked at the very beginning. Jesus wants all of his children to be loving. Where do we begin to love as Jesus would have us love? Jesus gives us the answer in our Gospel lesson for today. If we want to be loving, we must begin by loving God with all our heart and with all our soul and with all our mind. Jesus said that is the most important commandment of them all. That is where true Christian love begins. If we do that first, then it will also be possible for us to love our neighbor as ourselves.

When we think of all the good things God does for us and gives us, that is not hard to do. So go, my young friends, and love the Lord your God with all your heart and with all your soul and with all your mind. That is where true Christian love begins. **— D. H.**

Sunday between October 30 and November 5 inclusive, Proper 26

NOV. 3, 1996   OCT. 31, 1999   NOV. 3, 2002

The Gospel: Matthew 25:1-13

Focus: Because we don't know when the Lord will come again, we must be ready at all times for his glorious return.

Experience: You and the children will talk about how we know when various events will take place in our lives. Some examples are Christmas, a person's birthday, and the time that church service begins. We can prepare for these events if we know when they will occur. No one knows, however, when Jesus will come again, so we must always be ready.

Preparation: Bring a calendar and a clock.

Come, Lord Jesus

IN NOT TOO MANY WEEKS *(mention how many weeks)* we will be celebrating the birth of our Lord Jesus Christ as a baby in Bethlehem. What do we call that special celebration? *(Responses.)* That's right, we call it Christmas. When I was your age, I would take a calendar, like this one, and mark off the days until Christmas. Who can tell me what the date for Christmas is? *(Responses.)* Yes, Christmas comes every year on December 25.

If we have a calendar and we know the date of an event, such as Christmas, we get ready to celebrate it. What other special holidays can you think of that we might find on a calendar? *(Responses. On your calendar, locate the date of each holiday mentioned.)* This is another important date for me. *(Point to the date for your own birthday.)* Why do you suppose it is important? *(Responses.)* You guessed it, this is my birthday. Does anyone here have a birthday coming up soon? *(Responses.)* When is your birthday? That is only *(number of)* days from now. My guess is that your parents, since they know the date, too, are probably already making preparations for the big event.

Sometimes it is not only important to know the date of an event but also the time that event is to take place. Sunday is the day we have church, but you also need to know what time Sunday school and the church service begin. What do you have to look at to make certain you get to church on time? *(Responses.)* That's right, you use a clock or watch to tell what time it is. By looking at the clock, you can discover how much time you have to prepare for going to church, or school, or wherever you need to be.

We use calendars and clocks to measure time. They work well as we prepare to do things and go places. It is hard to be prepared for an event or activity, however, if we don't know when it will happen. Jesus told his disciples that one day he would come back to earth. The problem is, we don't know when that will happen. How should we, as God's children, prepare for our Lord's return?

The answer to this question is really quite simple. We should live every day as if it is the one when the Lord is going to come back. Begin each day by asking the Lord to help you live as one of his children. Ask God to forgive your sins for Jesus' sake. Finally, as we wait for the Lord to return, let us tell others about Jesus and his great love for them. We may not know when Jesus will return, but we do know that when he does return, he will take us to heaven to be with him forever. Won't that be a wonderful day! **— D. H.**

The Gospel: Matthew 25:14-30

Focus: God blesses us with gifts and talents and expects us to make use of them.

Experience: You will begin by sharing a story about a gift that was not used and appreciated and continue by pointing out that God has blessed each of us with special gifts and talents. In addition, God has given us all the wonderful gift of his Word. Conclude by emphasizing that it is God's desire that we use the gifts he has given us for the good of others.

Preparation: If you use the story given here, you may wish to bring along a framed painting.

The Gifts of God

HOW MANY OF YOU ENJOY RECEIVING GIFTS? *(Allow for responses.)* Almost everyone likes to receive gifts. This morning we are going to talk about some of the wonderful gifts or talents that God gives to each of us. First, however, I would like to tell you a story about a gift that was given but not used. *(You may wish to substitute an incident from your own experience.)*

One day a woman came into my office at church. She had been blessed by God with the ability to paint beautiful pictures. With her she brought a picture that she had painted that she wanted me to have as a gift. She thought the picture would look great on my office wall. I thanked her for the gift, but since I did not have a hammer or nail to put the picture up, I thought I would wait until later to do it. I was very busy the next several days and forgot all about hanging the picture on the wall.

The woman returned to my office a week later to see where I had hung the picture she had given me. She was very disappointed to find that I had not taken the time to hang the picture. I felt bad that I had not used the wonderful gift she had given me. I learned a valuable lesson; gifts are not only to be appreciated but, more importantly, they are to be used.

Did you know that God has given each of you wonderful gifts and talents? You are all very young and may not yet know all the special talents you have. Some of you may be able to sing well, others may able to paint beautiful pictures, like the woman in the story. Still others of you may be really good at sports. There may be some of you here who have the talent of building things. We could go on and on mentioning the talents that you may have.

Whatever talents we might have, one thing is clear: God wants us to make use of them. He wants us to use them not only for our own good but also for the good of others. In addition to the talents God has given us, there is one gift that he has given to all of us. That is the wonderful gift of his Word, the Bible. Like our talents, this is one gift that he wants us to make use of ourselves. We use this special gift most wisely when we share it with others.

One of the questions God might ask each of us when we get to heaven is, "What did you do with all those wonderful gifts and talents that I gave to you?" I hope that we will all be able to say that we used those gifts and shared them with others. Then our Lord will say, "Well done, my good and faithful servant!" **— D. H.**

Sunday between November 13 and 19 inclusive, Proper 28

The Gospel: Matthew 23:1-12

Focus: Jesus not only talked about serving others, he did it all of his life. Out of his great love for us, he gave up the bliss of heaven, took on the role of a servant, and died so that we might have eternal life. His desire for his children is that they will love as he loved and serve as he served.

Experience: You and the children will begin with a simple game of "Follow the Leader." There will be a slight twist in the game, however, in that while you tell the children to do one motion, you always do a different motion. Compare this to some of the Pharisees; Jesus told his disciples not to act like them. Finally, Jesus' desire for his children, that they love and serve others, will be emphasized.

Humble Servants

THIS MORNING I WOULD LIKE TO BEGIN our time together with a little game of "Follow the Leader." Would you all please stand? Now listen carefully and do exactly what I tell you to do. Put your hands on your head. *(Place your hands on your hips.)* Fold your hands and place them in front of you. *(Fold your hands and place them behind you.)* Take your hands and cover your ears. *(Cover your eyes with your hands.)* *(By now there will be some protests, but continue anyway.)* Place your hands on your knees. *(Place your hands on your shoulders.)* How did we do with our game of "Follow the Leader"? *(Responses.)*

I'm glad that some of you noticed I never did any of the motions that I asked you to do. It was rather confusing, wasn't it, especially if you were watching me as you listened. In order to succeed, you had to listen to what I said and ignore what I did.

In our Gospel lesson for today Jesus warned his disciples about some of the Pharisees who were the church leaders of his day. He told his disciples that it was all right to listen to what those Pharisees said, but not to do what they did. The Pharisees were like *I* was in our game of "Follow the Leader." *(Review what you did.)* They told the people what to do but they didn't do it themselves. In fact, some of the Pharisees were show-offs who only did things so people would see how good they were. They thought they were better than other people and loved all the praise and attention they received from others.

Jesus talked a lot about loving and serving others. But Jesus was not like those Pharisees. Jesus did what he said. Jesus spent his whole life helping others. He did this because he loved them. He loved people so much that he was willing to die on the cross to take away the guilt of their sins. Jesus told his disciples, and that includes us, that we should follow his example. As his children we are to share his love both by what we say and, just as importantly, by what we do. What are some good and helpful things you can do? *(Responses. They may mention helping their parents, picking up toys, not fighting, and so forth.)*

Those are all good things. We are to love and serve our neighbors, not so that others will say how great we are, but as a way to say thank you to Jesus for all that he did and continues to do for us. **— D. H.**

Christ the King,
Sunday between November 20 and 26 inclusive,[*]
Proper 29

The Gospel: Matthew 25:31-46

Focus: Whenever we do acts of kindness for others, it is just as if we had done them for Jesus.

Experience: You and the children will explore what they would be willing to do for Jesus if he came to visit in person. Whenever we do kind acts for those in need, it is just as if we had done them for Jesus himself.

For Jesus' Sake

ISN'T IT WONDERFUL TO HAVE A FRIEND LIKE JESUS? He loved us all so much that he was willing to suffer death on the cross and rise again for our salvation. I'm really looking forward to meeting Jesus face to face so I can thank him for his great love for me.

Let's pretend this morning that Jesus has come to visit us in person. He would probably walk in and greet all of us very warmly. Then as he spoke with us, let's imagine that he says, "I certainly am hungry." What do you suppose you would want to do? *(Responses.)* That's right. You would want to get him something to eat. You would probably try to get him food that he really enjoys. I can't imagine that any of us would either ignore him or refuse to get him something to eat.

Imagine that he then says, "I am very thirsty. Something cold to drink would certainly taste good right now." What would you do? *(Responses.)* That's right, we would get him a cold drink. As he continues talking with us, he mentions that the robe he is wearing is old and worn out. What do you suppose you would do? *(Responses.)* Getting him a new robe sounds like a good idea.

I have some exciting news to share with you! We have an opportunity to take care of Jesus' needs almost every day. Any time we give food to someone who is hungry, or a drink to someone who is thirsty, or clothing to someone who needs them, or when we visit someone who is sick or in prison or lonely, Jesus says it is just as if we had done it for him. We said that we would do

---

[*] Last Sunday after Pentecost

things for Jesus because of his great love for us. Jesus now says to us, "Love one another just as I have loved you."

Can you think of some things you can do, or your family can do, or our church can do to help people? *(Responses. Help them identify food shelves, clothing drives, and individual actions that help others.)* When we help someone in need we show our love not only for them but also for Jesus. That is just the way in which Jesus would have us respond to his great love for us. **— D. H.**

The Gospel: Luke 17:11-19

Focus: Giving thanks to God is something we should remember to do every day.

Experience: You and the children will begin with a discussion of the variety of ways that people show their thankfulness. Then you will discuss when we should be thankful and what God would have us be thankful for.

Preparation: Bring a thank-you card to show the children. Also bring a personal item that was given to you by another as an expression of thanks.

Thanksgiving Every Day

THE OTHER DAY I RECEIVED THIS CARD IN THE MAIL. What are the two words on the front of this card? *("Thank you".)* That's right, this is a thank-you card. When I opened the envelope and saw the words on the card, I knew right away that someone wanted to thank me for something I had said, done, or given. Thanking others is something we do, or should do, quite often.

Sending thank-you cards is only one of the ways one person can tell another, "Thanks." What is another way to do it? *(We can call them or talk to them.)* Yes, we can simply say the words "Thank you" to someone else. Some people just say, "Thanks," others say, "Thanks a lot" or "Thanks very much." If you are refusing a kind offer, you might say, "No, thanks."

Take a look at what I have in my hand. *(Show the personal item given you as a gift.)* This was given to me by someone as a way of saying "Thank you" for something I did for them. Giving gifts to others is yet another way of saying "Thank you" to them. You can also thank others by patting them on the back, shaking their hands, or giving them a big hug.

No matter how we do or say it, we usually give thanks for something good that has been given us, told us, or done for us. It is our way of letting other people know that we appreciate or feel good about something that has happened.

Have you ever said "Thank you" and not really meant it? *(Responses.)* For example, maybe you say "Thank you" when your teacher hands you back a paper and it has red check marks for things you did wrong. Or you may say "Thank you" to someone who has just served you food that you don't like very well.

Then there are those occasions when you forget to say "Thank you" and a stern look crosses Mom's or Dad's face as they say those familiar words, "And what are you supposed to say?"

God has something rather interesting to say about when we should be thankful. We are supposed to give thanks in all circumstances, for the Bible says that *(read 1 Thessalonians 5:18)*. You will notice in this verse that God doesn't want us to give thanks only during good times, but at all times. This means, of course, that God wants us to be thankful even when things are not going so well for us. Knowing we have a heavenly Father who loves us can make any problem bearable and gives us a good reason for giving thanks.

What, then, should we be thankful for? *(Everything.)* If you guessed "everything," you are right. Listen to these words from the first letter to Timothy: "Everything that God has created is good: nothing is to be rejected but all is to be received with a prayer of thanksgiving" *(1 Timothy 4:4)*. God is the giver of good gifts.

I certainly hope that all of you have a blessed and happy Thanksgiving. Then the rest of the year, continue to be thankful for everything at all times, for this is the will of God. **— D. H.**